BIG Q
LITTLE Q
THE CALM BEFORE THE STORM...

By

a Friend of Medjugorje

By

A Friend of Medjugorje

CARITAS OF BIRMINGHAM
STERRETT, ALABAMA 35147 USA

Special Statement

Caritas of Birmingham is not acting on behalf of the Catholic Church or placing its mission under the church. Its mission is to reach all people of the earth. Its actions are outside of the church done privately. It is further stated:

So as not to take for granted the credibility of the Medjugorje Apparitions, it is stated that the Medjugorje apparitions are not formally approved by the Catholic Church.

Medjugorje Status

February 25, 2019 A.D.

No attempt is intended to pre-empt the Church on the validity of the Medjugorje Apparitions. They are private revelation waiting the Church's final judgment[1]. In the interim, these private revelations **are** allowed by, and for, the faithful to have devotion to and to be spread legally by the Church. Devotion and the propagation of private revelations can be forbidden only **if** the private revelation is condemned because of anything it contains which contravenes faith and morals according to AAS 58 (1966) 1186 Congregation for the Doctrine of the Faith. Medjugorje has not been condemned nor found to have anything against faith or morals, therefore it is in the grace of the Church to be followed by the faithful. By the rite of Baptism one is commissioned and given the authority to evangelize. *"By Baptism they share in the priesthood of Christ, in His prophetic and royal mission."*[2] One does not need approval to promote or to have devotions to private revelations or to spread them when in conformity to AAS 58 (1966) 1186, as the call to evangelize is given when baptized. These apparitions have not been approved formally by the Church. Caritas of Birmingham, the Community of Caritas and all associated with it, realize and accept that the final authority regarding the Queen of Peace, Medjugorje and happenings related to the apparitions, rests with the Holy See in Rome. We at Caritas, willingly submit to that judgment. While having an amiable relationship with the Diocese of Birmingham and a friendly relationship with its bishop, Caritas of Birmingham as a lay mission is not officially connected to the Diocese of Birmingham, Alabama, just as is the Knights of Columbus.[3] The Diocese of Birmingham's official position on Caritas is neutral and holds us as Catholics in good standing.

1. The Church does not have to approve the apparitions. The Church can do as She did with the apparitions of Rue du Bac in Paris and the Miraculous Medal. The Church never approved these apparitions. She gave way to the people's widespread acceptance of the Miraculous Medal and thereby the Apparitions to St. Catherine. *Sensus Fidelium* (Latin, meaning "The Sense of the Faithful"), regarding Medjugorje, is that the "sense" of the people says that "Mary is here (Medjugorje)."
2. Catechism of the Catholic Church 2nd Edition
3. The Knights of Columbus also are not officially under the Church, yet they are very Catholic. The Knights of Columbus was founded as a lay organization in 1882, with the basic Catholic beliefs. Each local council appeals to the local Ordinary to be the Chaplain. The Knights of Columbus is still a lay organization, and operates with its own autonomy.

Published with permission from SJP Lic. COB.

ISBN: 978-1-878909-68-8

Printed and bound in the United States of America.

For additional copies, contact your local bookstore or call
Caritas of Birmingham at 205-672-2000 USA.

Or go to **mej.com** and click on *"Shop Online"*

Preface

A narrow view of the messages of the Virgin Mary, given through Her apparitions in Medjugorje,* minimizes the message. Our Lady has come to change the world. Her battle plan to conquer evil is Her messages. These messages, delivered by the Queen of Peace, are

* Explanation of the Apparitions of Medjugorje

In June 24, 1981, the Blessed Virgin Mary began appearing to six young people in former Yugoslavia, in a small village called Medjugorje. The Blessed Virgin Mary, known simply as Our Lady, began giving daily messages to the visionaries for the purpose of forming them into the spiritual life. In 1984, Our Lady told the visionaries that She would begin giving messages every Thursday to begin forming the parish of St. James Church in Medjugorje. In January, 1987, Our Lady then announced that Her weekly messages would end, but She would now begin giving monthly messages, every 25th, and that these messages were for the salvation of the whole world as they would lead the world back to Her Son.

The Medjugorje visionaries have been closely studied and scrutinized by scientists, psychologists, theologians, reporters as well as having to live under a microscope in their very public lives for nearly 40 years. But it is the scientists, some of whom were non-believers or atheists, who offer the most conclusive evidence that the six visionaries are truly experiencing supernatural apparitions from Heaven. (https://www.medjugorje.com/medjugorje/scientific-studies.html)

For over three decades, a Friend of Medjugorje has received from Our Lady what others have not understood. Throughout his 33 year involvement with Medjugorje, no one has been as bold or taken the risks he has taken in defining Medjugorje as the most important spiritual event in the history of the world since Christ's Death, Resurrection, Ascension, and the Descent of the Holy Spirit birthing the Church. He knew this in his heart and proclaimed it from the beginning. Now, beginning just in 2018, many are finally following his lead of where Our Lady has placed him, especially in teaching the world how to take the messages of Our Lady from the spiritual realm and put them into life in the physical realm. He is recognized around the world, as understanding Medjugorje as no one else has grasped. He will be known in history as the one Our Lady used to unlock Her messages for the world. First, in witnessing with his life the messages of Medjugorje that Our Lady called him to, and secondly through his writings.

from the spiritual realm which teaches and encompasses everything that happens in the physical world, EVERY THING. We see a plague in the world of Medjugorje that does not allow the passage of the message into EVERY THING in the physical world. There are plenty of such mentalities that prevail in the world of Medjugorje. While they would say this is not so, reality tells this truth.

These are tiny mentalities, very narrow and closed. They accept what they want to hear and reject, ignore or limit the messages' meaning in what they do not want to hear. It is why Our Lady said:

February 2, 2011

> **"...You listen to me while I am speaking to you, but your hearts are closed and you are not hearing me..."**

One has to open themselves up, look into the messages and every single aspect of life and how we live it. What is "it"? It is **"every word."** That is how important Our Lady's words are; even every "individual" word in every message has meaning and is strategically placed. Our Lady says:

June 25, 2002

"...Live my messages and put into life every word that I am giving you..."

Everyone has underestimated the importance of Our Lady's words. We, from the voice and chair Our Lady has granted us to have, here at Caritas, trumpet the messages' importance far beyond any part of the Medjugorje world. There is no avenue that is not to be touched by the messages, that is not to be changed and be stolen from the worldly and placed under the spiritual. This book will cover things that some mentalities will not be able to understand. It is not stated that what you are about to read is precise in detail as to what may happen in the future, but it has lessons to help you think for yourself, research for yourself and identify where the world is headed. Medjugorje visionary, Mirjana, wrote in 2016, in regards to the secrets:

"...I can only hint at what our future holds, but I do see indications that the events are already in motion. Things are slowly starting to develop. As Our Lady says, look at the signs..."

Nobody can prophesy exactly, but you can learn enough through the messages to see the direction. This writing will help you on that path and broaden the narrow mentalities of Medjugorje people and priests that are out there that kill Our Lady's plans because of such mentalities. All the while thinking that Our Lady is just asking for a few basic things in changing one's life. Our Lady is looking for a purification of mentalities and the world will not change until we open our hearts to Her. The vastness of which She is calling us to respond to is way beyond what anyone can imagine, including even the visionaries. That is why She seriously says for us to pray three hours a day because the walls of narrow mentalities must be broken down through trumpets of prayer, as the walls of Jericho were broken down at the sound of the "Trump"ets.

Friend of Medjugorje
March 6, 2019

ACKNOWLEDGEMENT

God alone deserves the credit for the publication of this book. It is from Him that the messages are allowed to be given through Our Lady to all of mankind. He alone deserves the praise and honor.

Table of Contents

* * * * * * A SPECIAL NOTE * * * * * *

In our books and newsletters, we have often recommended praying to the Holy Spirit for understanding. Turn off your phones and allow for no interruptions while you read. It has been proven that one interruption makes a person lose up to 50% of their concentration and memory. As you read this, become part of it. This book was not written to be read one time only. It is to be read several times. Each time it is read, you will gain more understanding than the previous reading. The Holy Spirit will provide the necessary enlightenment and understanding.

"We must be just as vigilant, committed and united in prayer and action as those who are doing everything in their power to bring down the United States. Faith, trust, prayer, unity—this is what draws the heart of God towards us and what presses Him to answer our prayers."[1]

Friend of Medjugorje
"Darkness is Fighting Against the Light"
April 2018

CHAPTER ONE

"We Conquer the Unknown"

On February 5, 2019, President Donald Trump gave his State of the Union Address. Below is a segment from his address that will be referenced throughout the coming pages, because in studying it, there are things that one can learn about Our Lady and Her plans:

> *"When American soldiers set out beneath the dark skies over the English Channel in the early hours of D-Day, 1944, they were just young men of 18 and 19, hurtling on fragile landing crafts, towards the most momentous battle in the history of war. Why did they do it? They did it for America. They did it for us. Together, we represent the most extraordinary*

nation in all of history. What will we do with this moment? How will we be remembered? Our most thrilling achievements are still ahead. Our most exciting journeys still await. Our biggest victories are still to come. We must choose whether we squander our great inheritance or whether we proudly declare that we are Americans. We do the incredible. We defy the impossible. ***We conquer the unknown****. This is the time to reignite the American imagination. This is the time to search for the tallest summit and set our sights on the brightest star. This is the time to re-kindle the bonds of love and loyalty and memory that link us together as citizens, as neighbors, as patriots. This is our future, our faith and our choice to make. I am asking you to choose greatness. No matter the trials we face; no matter the challenges to come, we must go forward together. We must keep America first in our hearts. We must* *keep freedom alive in our souls and we must always keep faith in America's destiny. That one nation, under God, must be the hope and the promise and the light and the glory among all the nations of the world. Thank you, God bless you and God bless America."*

President Donald Trump,
February 5, 2019

* * * * * * * * * * * *

With careful reflection and observation one can see we are in a stupendous moment. Is President Trump exaggerating what he says, in speaking of the Normandy Invasion, that it parallels this moment in the same way? He said Normandy was the greatest battle of war, **ever**. In his State of the Union Address, he makes the comparison that what we are facing today is something like the Normandy Invasion. One may say that is an exaggeration, but you won't think that when you have finished reading these pages. There are unknown things happening today that are far greater than what is known. President Trump refers to the unknown in his above speech. *"We conquer the unknown,"* he said, referring to what is happening right now, because there are things being done that are not known completely. These pages are going to shine light upon events of our day to show you that Our Lady is the center of all the activity taking place.

"We have lost our sense of sin! Today a slick campaign of propaganda is spreading an inane (empty; void) defense of evil, a senseless cult of satan, a mindless desire for transgression, a dishonest and frivolous freedom, exalting impulsiveness, immorality and selfishness as if they were new heights of sophistication."[2]

Pope Benedict XVI
Good Friday, 2006

CHAPTER TWO

"This is the Time"

When you enter onto the freeway, you go down the ramp, you pick up speed and you are paralleling traffic on the interstate. At a point, you will merge in with the other cars going down the freeway. There are two things about to merge together that are right now going parallel to each other:

1. The events of the world
2. The apparitions of Our Lady of Medjugorje.*

The two are coming closer and closer together and will eventually merge together. You just read President Trump saying three times in his State of the Union Address:

* See Preface, pg iii, Explanation of the Apparitions of Medjugorje

*"This is the **time**...This is the **time**...This is the **time**."*

Our Lady says:

January 25, 1987

"...This time is my time..."

And She has repeatedly said so. Can this be by chance? Our Lady says:

September 2, 2016

"...Nothing is by chance..."

Things unknown are becoming more visible. Our Lady just recently said:

October 2, 2018

"...evil which is all the more visible..."

We have a huge monster that is becoming more visible by the day. In regards to Normandy, the generals wanted to plan their attack as early as 1942. They were thinking about this for a long time. There were a lot of strategies that had to be planned; a lot of unknown things had to be talked about. As events unfolded in the war, they finally committed to the Normandy Invasion that took place in June 1944.

There was extensive planning for D-Day. The coordination of 5,500 ships, almost 30,000 planes, and 170,000 soldiers took months of preparation, in advance. The total number of men, soldiers and officers involved in the Battle of Normandy, and the support behind it, was more than 2,800,000 over a span of three weeks.[3] It was a huge undertaking. But what must be realized is that *Our Lady is here for something that big right now.* Our Lady said on August 2, 2011:

> **"...As individuals, my children, you cannot stop the evil that wants to begin to rule in this world and to destroy it..."**

Do you believe the apparitions of Our Lady in Medjugorje? Then you have to believe the messages, and if you believe the messages, you have to believe that satan is trying to rule the world to destroy it. This is what is happening right now, and there is a Normandy Invasion being planned right now against a diabolical threat over the whole world. What will be covered in these pages is, in many ways, tied to the messages. You can, through prayer, see that all events in the world are coming through Medjugorje. Why? Because we are in the midst of Divine Intervention. But Our Lady said:

August 2, 2011

> **"...the evil that wants to begin to rule in this world..."**

How can we be certain that evil will rule? Because Our Lady, six months later, after saying, **"...evil that wants to begin to rule...,"** said:

February 2, 2012

"...pride has come to rule..."

August 2, 2011 – **"wants."** February 2, 2012 – **"has come."**

Medjugorje is Our Lady's Central Headquarters—the Pentagon—in this war against evil. Our Lady has to have both, Her actors—those who are playing out certain significant roles within the events of our day, and Her apostles—those who are aligned with the Queen's plans to lead the world to conversion and salvation. Not everyone involved in implementing Her plans are apostles of Our Lady. Some, like Trump, are actors—they who have a great role and are important to the success of Her plan. Her plan also includes those who, since their birth, have been groomed for their part throughout their whole lives. They do not necessarily know Our Lady is behind what they are inspired to do, but they will find the strength within themselves to fight through to win this battle.

Our Lady has Her plans, through man, but She also has opposition.

July 12, 1984

> **"...These days satan wants to frustrate my plans. Pray that his plan not be realized..."**

There is a great battle going on, as we know from Our Lady's August 2, 1981, message:

> **"...A great struggle is about to unfold. A struggle between my Son and satan. Human souls are at stake."**

The spiritual realms of Heaven and hell, which we can't see, are in battle, but they fight their battle physically through man. The actors guided by Light and apostles of Our Lady are on one side, and the actors guided by darkness and demons of satan are on the other side. The two sides have already begun to engage. The dark side is going to be broadsided by the Light, especially when the three secrets are released,* just like what happened in the Normandy Invasion. When the Allies landed in Normandy, the Germans weren't expecting the attack to take place there. Medjugorje is an unlikely place to start a war between Christ and lucifer. Just as the Germans were deceived because the Allies set up a decoy to divert the German's attention to another place, Our Lady didn't go to Rome, didn't go to some extraordinary special place. Our Lady went to a most unlikely place, in a Communist country. In war, you must be covert. That is one of the rules of war.

* Our Lady revealed to the Medjugorje visionaries that there would be three admonitions sent to the earth that will prove Her apparitions in Medjugorje are real and that will cause a great tsunami of grace that will lead to the world's conversion and salvation. Our Lady told Medjugorje visionary, Mirjana, that when the first secret takes place, satan's power will be destroyed. The visionaries know what events will take place and the exact dates they will happen, and the events will be announced three days before they will occur. In 2016, Mirjana wrote that we have moved into the time of the secrets.

"Prayer is forcing evil to come out in the open, show its shameful face—and simultaneously, God is raising His army to fight this evil, through Our Lady, paralleling those growing in holiness with those growing in hatred, dividing the two as they grow and eventually will clash; one crushing the other in victory." [4]

A Friend of Medjugorje
"Two Americas," 2004

CHAPTER THREE

Physical Reality in the Spiritual Realm

In this moment, there has been something happening that, for a long time, was very covert, but that is now manifesting. As already alluded to, as evil manifests and becomes more visible so will a plan, like the Normandy invasion, evolve to stop evil's progression. The purpose of this book is to make known something that is very fascinating, even astounding. Heaven is moving believers to confront the devil with the power of God, and the numbers joining this movement are increasing everyday. Our Lady said on September 2, 1981:

"...The devil tries to reign over the people. He takes everything into his hands, but the

force of God is more powerful and God will conquer."

Do you realize where we are and what is happening? 's'atan* is building the antichrist system. It is stated that the system is almost complete, except there is one problem for the devil. What is it? The problem for the devil is that Our Lady is here to crush his head, to strike a mortal wound to his head. Genesis 3:15 says:

"I will put enmities between you and the woman, and thy seed and Her seed.[5] She shall crush thy head and thou shalt lie in wait for Her heel."

* 's' - A Friend of Medjugorje does not capitalize satan's name. He stopped 25 years ago. Why? satan does not deserve respect or honor when references are made to him. For years he has not capitalized satan's name because we all should refuse to give him this honor or recognition. Why should the application of grammar rules apply to him who has an insatiable desire to be exalted, above God? We refrain in our references and writings from giving him the same stature afforded even a dog's name. We are not radical in that we don't tell others they must do the same. It's up to each individual to decide for themselves. For the harm he has done to man, whom he despises, we will not grant him that which is even reserved for a dog.

This verse was stated as above for over one thousand years of Christianity, from its origin, and was later changed from ***"She shall crush thy head,"*** to *"he will crush his head."* Over time, man corrupts translations, especially modern scholars. There is a physical history of countless statues throughout the early centuries to now of the Virgin Mary standing on the head of the serpent. Christians have, from the earliest ages of Christianity, understood that the Virgin Mary would come to crush satan's head. For Christ to come and crush satan's head would only inflate satan's pride. It would give him bragging rights that he battled one-on-one with God. But for satan to be crushed by the heel of a mere mortal creature, and a woman at that, is to hand satan the ultimate humiliation. The only humiliation greater would be to be defeated by the help of sinners like us. Hence, God's purpose in sending the Virgin Mary in this time, when satan has amassed so much power.

We can state in the unseen spiritual realm, that there is a face-off between two opposing forces on the battlefield. The Virgin Mary is at the helm on the side of Light. If you cannot see this in the spiritual realm, then go in the physical realm to see it. Sr. Lucia,* one of three children to receive apparitions of the Virgin Mary in Fatima, Portugal, in 1917, said that the Second World War was a satanic war against the Jews, because even though they rejected Christ, they are still God's people and, therefore, a target of satan. Our Lady said:

January 2, 2017

> **"... My Son was the source of love and light when He spoke on earth to the people of all peoples..."**

* The Blessed Mother appeared to Lucia, and her two young cousins, Francesco and Jacinta, for six consecutive monthly visits, from May 13, 1917 until October 13, 1917. The Blessed Mother revealed many things to them and gave them three secrets, that have all been revealed, concerning future events. What was revealed in these secrets connects deeply with the battles we are experiencing in our time..

This was something Our Lady revealed to Lucia. The devil manifests his plans through his minions. World War II was the physical manifestation of a war taking place in the spiritual realm. Our Lady, from the spiritual realm, is manifesting Her battle plans, through us, in the physical realm today. She says:

July 3, 2009

"...be my extended hands."

We literally are being led by Heaven, we, the extended hands of Our Lady. This is not the first time in history this has happened. In the 1400s, Joan of Arc was used, and led spiritually by Heaven at the age of 15, to save France in the physical realm. When seeking the secret of her successes, Joan revealed that St. Michael the Archangel had taught her about battle, war and how to fight her enemies to prepare her for what God was going to call her to do. All this was in the spiritual realm. Joan, therefore, gives proof the spiritual realm is at work, at a high level of intervention in the physical realm.

What is the proof? How is it possible that a young, illiterate, peasant girl, whose only work was that of a seamstress, was taught military tactics unlike anything used in that time? Then, in just two years, was raised to become the Commander and Chief of the entire military of a major country at the age of 17. And, as the Commander and Chief, she brought an end to what was called the 100 Year War between England and France. These facts bring us back to the question, how is this possible to achieve without the aid of the supernatural? There is no other possible explanation than God was with Joan and led her to victory over and over again.

France had been reduced to holding onto only a few square miles. France was about to be no more. Joan of Arc was able to unite three rough and tough, much older generals who were quarrelling and divided among themselves. They saw Joan had a useful purpose in unifying and building confidence among the soldiers, but they thought it laughable that any of her military tactics would work. They, after all, were the generals and experts in war. Joan of Arc soon proved them wrong. The generals had tried to circumvent her orders. They wanted to do the 'same ole thing' they had always been doing. She overcame their resistance to her strategies that she had learned from the spiritual realm. When she demanded that her instructions be followed, they saw such success, that the three generals fell completely in submission to Joan.

Immediately going into battle, Joan began defeating the English after 100 years of fighting. The English began losing battle after battle. She saved France and the King's crown. Soon after, Joan was caught by the English, tried and burned at the stake. Her recorded trial is the oldest and best preserved recording of a trial in history.[6] Mark Twain was so taken by the story of Joan of Arc that he wrote one of the best books about her life. It was the only book that he did not want money for. He wanted Joan's true story known. He states at the end of his book:

> *"Taking into account, as I have suggested before, all the circumstances—her origin, youth, sex, illiteracy, early environment, and the obstructing conditions under which she exploited her high gifts and made her conquests in the field and before the courts that tried her for her life—she is easily and by far the most extraordinary person the human race has ever produced."* [7]

Louis Kossuth, known as the Father of Hungarian Democracy, stated of Joan of Arc:

> *"Consider this unique and imposing distinction. Since the writing of human history began, Joan of Arc is the only person, of either sex, who has ever held supreme command of*

the military forces of a nation ***at the age of seventeen.***" [8]

Joan's life is important to study because it can only be explained by the spiritual realm acted out in the physical realm.

It has been said:

"In the centuries that have elapsed, since Joan of Arc, five hundred millions of Frenchmen have lived and died blessed by the benefactions of her life and battles conferred and so long as France shall endure, the mighty debt must grow." [9]

If there had been no Joan of Arc, there would be no France. France would not exist today.

If there was no Donald Trump, there would be no United States of America in the future. The United States will cease to exist if Trump is not successful.

One thing they had in common, people loved them or hated them

We are in different times, where different tactics must be employed to fight our enemies. Heaven was active in France's continuation and Heaven is active today in America's continuation. There is a physical reality to these messages of the Virgin Mary, who has come to teach us how to fight evil.

In addition, there exists a provable physical reality that confirms the spiritual realm of the Medjugorje apparitions. Twenty-plus scientists, over a span of 22 years, found in the results of hundreds of scientific tests they administered on the six visionaries of Medjugorje, that they are, in fact, seeing a supernatural event in front of them. The final unanimous determination by the scientists' was that the six visionaries are:

"ABSENT OF DECEIT."[10]

Therefore, we cannot think that our only responsibility is to just go to Medjugorje, just go to church, just fast, just pray and read spiritual books. No, all of these spiritual works are to result in something else. We are to engage in a battle—a great battle between Heaven and hell. It is a battle between the minions of satan, who are real people on the side of darkness, against the masses of us who are on the side of Light. However, we may think, *"Oh, but we are in the Light,"* which is dangerous thinking. It is an attitude of self-righteousness that will not help us to win this battle. Our disposition must be wanting God's plans to manifest for the salvation of the world, for the good of all man. Any other motivation will cause us to lose.

Before going into the logistics that are taking place, don't pass this off, saying, *"Oh this is just politics. I don't need to know these things. I only want to hear the messages."* You are way down at a kindergarten level with the messages if that is what you think. On June 23, 2017, in a recent message, Our Lady said:

> **"...Fight against evil..."**

Yes, pray. Yes, go to church. Yes, read the Bible— but these are the means to gain the strength for the battle. We are in battle. We are to fight. Continuing with Our Lady's June 23, 2017, message, She says:

> **"...Fight against evil and against sin and the idols of today's world which seduce you..."**

"For evil to secure itself, its ability to continue to rule, it must make radical moves now while it has its foot in the door. The intention of those on the verge of consolidating their power is to push for it now, knowing that once their evil intentions are exposed, to retreat is to face defeat. Evil must make its moves now because Christians and people of good will are waking up. Those who possess evil intentions which rule in their hearts, have a limited time to make radical moves. The more moves they make, the more naked their intentions become and, therefore, the quicker they must move to the next step, in order to bulldoze resistance before it builds any momentum to resist and stop them." **[11]**

A Friend of Medjugorje
They Fired the First Shot
2012

CHAPTER FOUR

Be Hot or Cold

The Democratic Party is evil. Its platform is evil. You cannot be a Democrat or vote for a Democrat and be a Christian at the same time. Why? Voting for any Democrat means you are endorsing what they stand for—which is defined in the Democratic Platform. It is the Democratic Party that is fighting for the right to kill babies after they have been born—infanticide. On February 25, 2019, a bill to protect babies, who are born alive, from being killed was voted down by virtually every Democrat. The Republican Platform is a good document and it has good principles, but some of the establishment members of the Republican Party are just as bad as the Democrats. In fact, they are worse. Jesus said that in the Book of Revelation:

> ***"I know your deeds, that you are neither cold nor hot. I wish you were either one or the other! So, because you are lukewarm—neither hot nor cold—I am about to spew you out of my mouth."*** Rev. 3:15-17

Be hot or cold. If you are in the middle, Christ will spew you out of His mouth, or in other words, ***"I will vomit you out of my mouth."*** Actually, the Democrats get more respect from God in the fact that they say who they are and what they stand for and act accordingly. Whereas there are Republicans who pretend they are one thing, but in reality, they are just as corrupt as the Democrats. So, we don't have a situation of Democrats vs. Republicans. We have a situation of Democrats and some Republicans vs. the Light. Yes, there are good Republicans, who abide by Christian principles and vote accordingly, but one must understand that today, the traditional lines of knowing who your enemies are has become very blurred. As Light increases and darkness is exposed, no doubt we will be shocked to find people, who we thought were on the side of Light, were really working for darkness, and vice versa. Before going further, it is important to lay the groundwork for you to understand what is about to be explained.

We have in our government five different classes of security clearances. They are listed as follows:[12]

1. **Confidential – Level 1**, has two classifications of documents that can be seen under its security clearance.

2. **Secret – Level 2**, has four classifications of documents that can be seen under its security clearance.

3. **Low Level – Level 3**, has six classifications of documents that can be seen under its security clearance.

4. **Top Secret – Level 4**, also has six categories of documents, but the information is higher level

than what is found in lower classes of intelligence.

5. **"Q" Clearance—Level 5, is the top level of security**. It has access to all levels of clearance, 10 categories, which includes National Security Special and Critical Sensitive information. These individuals hold positions of *"extraordinary accountability because 'the secrets they know harness the potential to cause* ***exceptionally grave*** *or* ***inestimable*** *damage' to the national security of the United States of America."* [13] When you hear the word "Q Clearance" you are at the top. You have access to what the President knows and the highest levels of the military.

Why is that important to understand? Because it is part of the plan of Our Lady to combat against satan whom She says:

December 25, 1990

"...wants to destroy my plans..."

Do you respond, *"Our Lady wouldn't get involved in war?"* Really? You've read Joan of Arc. There are things in history that many believe to be Divine Intervention. There were known miracles within the invasion of Normandy. Fog hid planes and ships from view until the attack was underway. Believing that the Allied forces would never chance crossing the English Channel in stormy weather, the Germans were lulled into complacency and the Allies were able to achieve maximum surprise in their attack once they hit the Normandy shores. The soldiers believed God was providing the perfect conditions to give them the upper hand in the fierce battle ahead.

General Eisenhower, after seeing the results of his decision to initiate the invasion, though the weather conditions were risky to do so, stated, *"If there was nothing else in my life to prove the existence of an almighty God, the events of the next 24 hours did it."*[14] Not only did God bring success to their enterprise, but they were able to bring the war to an end much sooner because of their victory on D-Day. If we walk in the Light, God will protect us and help us win our battles. Our Lady said on April 25, 1987:

> **"...pray that God's blessing may protect each one of you from all the evil that is threatening you..."**

President Trump said in the State of the Union Address, *"We defy the impossible. We conquer the unknown."* But how? We have threats against us that are **unknown**, that can only be conquered through prayer and fasting. Any other way is impossible. Prayer and fasting, which are operatives in the spiritual realm, will bring the graces necessary to those who, in the physical realm, are fighting on the front lines, and to us who are behind on the second front, to help us win this battle.

"Now is the moment to at least alter somewhat our present circumstances and change our future. If enough people change, greater will the future change by our decisions today. This is a grace period for us as Christians and all other people of good will. Our Lady comes to tell us to alter our future now in the present. Our Lady said:

June 15, 2012

> **"...Put...(God) in the first place in your life and in your families and together with Him, set out into the future...through this upcoming time of grace..."** [15]

A Friend of Medjugorje
They Fired the First Shot 2012

CHAPTER FIVE

In This Moment

In October 2017, the two realms merged together briefly—the spiritual and the physical—to reveal something astounding. Let's turn back the clock to October 2017. This is a significant time because it ties to the Virgin Mary and Fatima. October 13, 2017, was the 100th anniversary of the last Fatima apparition. There were many writings and broadcasts from here,* about this over the past several years, because this date marked the end of the 100 year reign of satan of which Our Lady had spoken to Medjugorje visionary, Mirjana Soldo. Do you think, after 100 years of his reign, that there would not be a profound meaning to everything that was happening in the world? Do you think Heaven was

* Caritas of Birmingham in Caritas, Alabama.

just idly standing by at that moment? Isn't it more likely that Heaven had been arranging and putting in place its own people for the moment when Our Lady's reign would begin, a reign that is meant to prepare the world for Her Son's final coming, be it 5 or 50 or 500 years from now?

Plans were being initiated right at the beginning—in October 2017. Is there something that happened in that month? We couldn't see, at that moment, what we are able to see now, 16 months later (as of March 1, 2019), but what is manifesting is astounding. We are starting to see the fingerprint of Our Lady as Her century begins.

In President Trump's State of the Union Address, many things he said are in the messages of Our Lady. He talked about **"this moment."** What moment are we in? We are in **"this time"** of Our Lady. So when he says, *"What will you do with this moment?"* Our Lady is telling us through the messages. ***"I'm telling you what to do in this moment.***

I'm telling you advance against satan. I'm telling you to change the world. I'm telling you to sacrifice yourself for the salvation of the world. Expose evil. Do battle against evil." So, let's uncover certain things. And again, you will see that what is happening in the **spiritual** realm will eventually manifest in the **physical** realm.

Something profound happened on October **5**, 2017, just before Our Lady's 100th anniversary of Her apparitions in Fatima. President Trump had a meeting in the White House with his top generals, the brightest generals in the world, those who could lay out a plan, those who could come up with a strategy.

What unfolded after the meeting was something unexpected. President Trump called the media in for a photo op. The generals, with their wives, lined up beside President Trump and his wife, Melania, as the room filled with flashes from cameras. Trump, talking to the press, says, *"You guys know what this represents?"* Not waiting for an answer, Trump says, *"Maybe it's the calm before the storm."* He then adds, *"Could be the calm, the calm before the storm."*

So, what does that mean? You have the top generals, the brightest minds, standing there, and he says, *"This is the calm before the storm."* Many wondered at the time if Trump was referring to North Korea. He had been challenging Kim Jong Un, calling his bluff, referring to him as Little Rocket Man, etc. Many thought Trump was speaking about North Korea when he said, "the calm before the storm." Trump, himself, may have even been thinking so. But when the spiritual realm is at play, one can say something for a purpose at hand, in the present, that will apply to something different in the future that is yet unknown.

Trump didn't say this by accident; he said it strategically. He was telling us something that we didn't know because it was **unknown** at that point.

We could conclude, at the time, that it was about North Korea, but now we know it is not completely the case, as it was only partially about that. As Trump continued with the photo op, smiling for the cameras, he said of his generals, *"We have the world's great military people in this room. I will tell you that."* One reporter shouted out, *"What storm, Mr. President?"*

Those words by the President had gotten their attention, along with all the optics that were present: the President with his generals standing around him, after having a special, private meeting that was out of character of a normal day. Then the President talked about *"the calm before the storm."* So, naturally a reporter would ask, *"What storm, Mr. President?"* Everybody wanted to know. How did Trump respond? He said, *"You'll find out."* That is all he said.

Again, that was October 5, 2017. This event was filled with so much intrigue. Yet, even at that time, no one had any idea of how big this really was. It is just now becoming clear. Trump, knowingly or unknowingly, was initiating a major strategy, that would lead this nation towards something like the Normandy Invasion. It may not be with troops. It may not be with ships, but it's something just as impacting in changing the world. Press Secretary Sarah Sanders was interviewed the following day, on October 6, 2017, the day after Trump made the *"calm before the storm"* statement. What follows is a portion of that transcript:

Reporter: *"Was President Trump referring to military action when he was referring to "the calm before the storm?"*

Press Secretary Sarah Sanders: *"We're never going to say, in advance, what the President is going to do."*

Reporter: *"How seriously should the American public or American adversaries for that matter take these comments, serious…"*

Press Secretary Sarah Sanders: *"I think you can take the President protecting the American people always extremely serious and if he feels that action is necessary, he'll take it."*

Trump, on October 6, 2017, was questioned again about his statement. One reporter called the *"calm before the storm"* statement an *"unsolicited **cryptic** comment."*

Reporter: *"Mr. President, what did you mean by "calm before the storm" yesterday? What did you mean by that?"*

President Trump: *"You'll find out."*

What did Trump mean when he said, *"You'll find out?"* Was he speaking about North Korea? At the time, it was thought so. But, no storm associated with North Korea materialized. Through Trump's diplomacy, the threat of North Korea lessened over time. Though it may still be a threat, Trump was able to let the steam out of the pressure cooker and begin the process of developing a relationship with North Korea's Kim Jong-Un in order to wield influence over him; something no other world leader was able to do. So, then, what storm was Trump referring to? And again, it must always be kept in mind the timing of this moment—right in the month when satan's 100 year reign ends and Our Lady's Reign begins, October 13, 2017. Was there something else that was going on in this moment?

"We need a new strategy against these advances. The attacks against our liberties and our faith are no longer being made just yearly or monthly or even daily, but now by the hour they march against us. These strategies we have been engaged in have been ineffective, and if we continue down this path, we will see the last vestige of Christian principles in our law and our way of life disappear, forcibly taken from us." [16]

Friend of Medjugorje
They Fired the First Shot 2012

CHAPTER SIX

Is This Just Another Conspiracy Theory?

The answer to the question ending the last chapter is, actually, yes. Just 15 days after the Fatima 100th anniversary date of October 13, 2017, something appeared on the horizon—noticed at first by only a small number. It appeared on October 28, 2017, on a type of Internet forum, popular for its anonymous users. It identified itself only as **"Q."** Q began posting a series of "**cryptic** messages" in a thread* entitled ***"Calm Before the Storm,"*** the same words Trump used on October 5, 2017, when gathered with his generals.

* In online discussions, a *thread* is a series of messages that have been posted as replies to each other. A single forum or conference typically contains many *threads*, covering different subjects. By reading each message in a *thread*, one after the other, you can see how the discussion has evolved.

Q claims to be a group of patriots in Military Intelligence/NSA with access to all the information, including Top Secret and Secret Restricted Data. Q stated on November 7, 2017:

"We serve at the pleasure of the President. DJT." [17]

On that October day in 2017, and up to this present time, Q has continually posted what he describes as "intel drops," meaning intelligence that only someone close to Trump could know, say those who follow Q's posts closely. People began to wonder if "Q" could be what Trump was referring to when he said, *"You'll find out."*

Followers of Q began to grow exponentially and, in just over 15 months, Q had become a worldwide phenomenon. TIME magazine reported that in the year 2018, **Q made the list of the top 25 Most Influential People on the Internet, worldwide.** This gave Q huge credibility to have this kind of following in just over one year of going online. Books are already being published about him. And though he is face-less and name-less, he is among the most attacked individuals in the mainstream media.

Who is Q? His identity is still a mystery. It could be a man or a small group of people, but what is generally accepted is that Q is believed to be military because his intel drops, what he calls "crumbs," are very coded. He has declared that the President of the United States has a master plan to stage a counter-coup against the members of the Deep State—those planted primarily in the top of the bureaucracy and the three-letter agencies, the FBI, CIA and NSA.*

One may say that "Q" is a conspiracy "pie in the sky" theory. But one cannot think the Deep State is a conspiracy. It is a fact. Obama, for eight years,

* FBI —Federal Bureau of Investigation
CIA —Central Intelligence Agency
NSA —National Security Agency

built the Deep State, appointing actors for his bidding to circumvent and subvert the government of the United States of America, against the people, to protect and hold onto his own power, and the power of those he is associated with. This is well known. If the counter-coup by President Trump is true, then this is a bombshell revelation. Q is dropping intel every day, giving hints and insights as to what is coming. Most people who follow Q think he is within the inner circle of the President and is revealing to the people what the President mentioned in the State of the Union Address, when he said:

"We conquer the unknown."

You may not think so. Again, you, yourself, may be thinking that Q is just another conspiracy theory. However, if Q is accurate in what he is saying, and there is a lot of evidence to say that he is, then what is coming, what is being planned, gives the appearance of a real coup d'état against those who are trying to usurp the United States government and destroy America. People have listened to Fake News too long. The truth is that we are too concerned with following a code of civility in speaking of "Fake News." Our Lady does not have such scruples. She speaks the truth. She says:

February 2, 2018:

"...My children, do not believe lying voices..."

Our Lady's words are much more truthful than saying, it is Fake News. If we call a spade a spade, we should change the term "~~Fake News~~" to "Lying Voices." However, we can discern truth by their lies. The Lying Voices tell us and show us every day their plan. It is no longer a hidden conspiracy. If there is going to be a counter-coup to darkness, who hates the Light, the Light must be covert in its work to rid evil. They kept Normandy a secret until the moment of the invasion. The intel drops that Q is putting out are very profound in what they say and are very logical and methodical. They are having a profound impact on both the side of Light and the side of darkness.

You read what Sarah Sanders said when she was questioned about the President. She said:

> *"I think you can take the President protecting the American people always extremely serious..."*

When individuals heard that, we all were thinking, solely, North Korea. But, as mentioned, the threat posed by North Korea has somewhat diminished over time. This was not true of the threat to the American people being perpetrated by renegades actively usurping the U.S. in order to destroy it.

We have an entrenched Deep State, a body of people that have been placed in government positions throughout our whole nation that are ready to transform the United States away from everything we were founded upon. This, again, is not a conspiracy theory. Just look at the news every day, if you can get past the ~~Fake News~~, Lying Voices,* to understand what is going on. As already mentioned, we have people, who hate this nation and what it stands for, who want it destroyed and who are doing everything they can to destroy it. Why? Because this Country is the only Country that can bring a moral order back to the whole world.

* A major part of the battle is verbiage. ~~Fake News~~ is not accurate. When they say their ~~Fake News,~~ and we know they are lying, we must call a spade, a spade. President Trump understands the importance of the verbiage war. He recently tweeted, from now on when he refers to our Country, he will capitalize the word. This is a positive attack against those who want our Country destroyed. Correct anyone who says ~~Fake News~~, that *"no, it is lying voices."*

To defeat this assault, Christians, and all people of good will, should have strategies to prevail in our faith and principles which are simple. No need for a complex formula. One goal, one aim. A strategy, like the heroic Christians of the past:

We win. They lose. Nothing less. [18]

Friend of Medjugorje
They Fired the First Shot 2012

CHAPTER SEVEN

Heaven's Covert Strategy

Heaven has a strategy that it employs when God decides to change things from darkness to Light. Do you want to know what that strategy is? Study how God grew and spread the Church 2,000 years ago. Some of Christ's apostles and disciples were drawn by the Holy Spirit to Greece, and from Greece and other places, to the Roman Empire. Paganism in Rome eventually fell and with it, spread Christendom throughout the veins of the world of the Roman Empire. Where is St. Peter buried? In the center of Rome. Where is St. Paul buried? In Rome. What does that say?

If you infiltrate the heart of paganism, and corruption, you birth Light from darkness, and you change the whole world. Through corrupted leaders, darkness has infiltrated major portions of our government and culture which spread throughout the states down to the major cities of the United States, which exported that **darkness** to change the world. However, that is where the Light is born. Our Lady's plans are to infiltrate with goodness the darkness within the United States, changing the world back towards goodness. The dynamic strategy of God, of how darkness gives birth to Light is illustrated in the following story by Jonathan Cahn, an inspired and prophetic author of our time:

> *"Come," said the teacher. "It's time for the lesson. We're going outside."*
>
> *I was half asleep and not thrilled at the idea, but, of course, I complied. He led me to a hill where we sat down in the darkness of the night.*

"Which comes first," he asked, "the day or the night?"

"The day," I answered. "Night comes when the day is over."

"That's what most people would say. And that's how most people in the world see it. Day leads into night. But it's not how God sees it."

"What do you mean?"

"If the day leads to night, then everything goes from light to darkness. Everything gets darker. Everything is in the process of darkening. And so is the way of the world. We go from day to night, from youth to aging, from strength to weakness, and ultimately from life to death. From day to night. It's the way of the world, but it's not the way of God. When God created the universe, it was not day and night. It is written, 'There was evening, and

then there was morning.' The day began with night. There was night and then there was day. In God, it is the night that comes first."

"So that's why Jewish holidays always begin at sunset."

"Yes, and not only Jewish holidays, but every Biblical day. Each day begins at sunset. There is evening and then morning. The world moves from day to night. But in God, it is the opposite. It goes from night to day... from darkness to light. The children of this world live from day to night. But the children of God live from night to day. They are born again in the darkness and move to the day. And if you belong to God, then that is the order of your life. You are to go from darkness to light, from weakness to strength, from despair to hope, from guilt to innocence, from tears to joy, and from death to life. And every night in your life will lead to the dawn. So live

according to God's sacred order of time...that your entire life be always moving away from the darkness and to the light."

As he said those words, the first light of the daybreak appeared and the night began yielding to the day." [19]

We are in the pains of darkness, birthing the Light of Truth. Our Lady of Medjugorje said:

September 25, 1998

"...you seek signs and messages and do not see that, with every morning sunrise, God calls you to convert and to return to the way of truth and salvation..."

Big Q

The godless media has done much to undermine our leaders and the security of our nation. We must attain wisdom through prayer and learn how to recognize truth. We must guard our information intake; look for direct sources from the event makers to make accurate judgments of events that take place in the world around us. Then we must shape our thinking and reasoning upon a Christian worldview.[20]

A Friend of Medjugorje
Look What Happened While You Were Sleeping
2007

CHAPTER EIGHT

The Secret Code to Conquer Evil

There is a great struggle over America and, thereby, a great struggle over the whole world. Just as Our Lady said:

August 2, 1981

> **"...A great struggle is about to unfold. A struggle between my Son and satan. Human souls are at stake."**

This struggle, in the spiritual realm, is manifesting in a physical struggle, the two paralleling each other in the events happening today. That is why we can proclaim, all the present and future events that will take place in the world are coming through Medjugorje, through the Queen of Peace. There are good actors and bad actors that are coming together in a clash.

In the spiritual realm, we have "Big Q," and in one significant aspect of the physical realm, we have "Little Q." Little does not mean weak, rather "Little Q" has might. The "Big Q" gives might. Our Lady said:

June 27, 1988

> **"…I give you might, dear children; with this might, you can bear everything. May this might make you strong in everything. You need it; that is why I give you might."**

Both Qs are revealing the battle plan through "intel drops," but Our Lady is dropping intel from Heaven. President Ronald Reagan learned of the apparitions of the Virgin Mary taking place in Medjugorje through his ambassador, Alfred Kingon. Kingon had visited Medjugorje and met Marija, one of the visionaries. It was suggested to

Marija to write a letter to President Reagan, which she did, expressing to him that Our Lady's purpose in coming to the world was for peace. Kingon personally delivered Marija's letter to Reagan, just before his meeting with Gorbechev in December 1987. When entering into the meeting, Reagan pulled Marija's letter out and told Gorbechev that the Virgin Mary was appearing in Yugoslavia for peace in the world. Reagan then said, *"That's what I'm here for."** So, "Big Q" is the Queen. The Queen of what? The Queen of Peace.

Who is "Little Q?" As already mentioned, Q may be a small group of military or other patriots close to President Trump; some even believe that President Trump occasionally makes an intel drop himself, his signature being Q+. What can be

* This story was told to a Friend of Medjugorje, by Medjugorje visionary, Marija, just after the Reagan/Gorbechev story happened. Marija and a Friend of Medjugorje met for the first time in July 1986. Their relationship grew quickly as it was ordained. He and his wife share an intimate history with Marija which opened, to a Friend of Medjuigorje, insights of Our Lady's apparitions that few have been exposed to

known is that those who are behind Q, or Q himself, are following a Biblical Strategy that defeated the enemies of God thousands of years ago in the story of Joshua in the Battle of Jericho.

What happened thousands of years ago is happening now. In the battle over Jericho, that is told in the book of Joshua, why didn't God just send Joshua straight to the walls of Jericho and attack their enemy who were protected behind the walls? Why, instead, did God tell Joshua to march around the city walls? Why then did God tell Joshua to march around the city every day for six days before attacking the city. Why was once around the walls not enough?

On the first day after God gave Joshua His instructions, Joshua and his men, 40,000 in number, marched around Jericho. The second day, they did it again. The third day, they did it again. What do you think was happening to those soldiers within the walls? Do you think they were wondering, *"What are these guys doing? This is getting a little bit unnerving. We're ready to fight them now. Why are they waiting?"* On the fourth day, it happens again, and on the fifth day, it happens again, and on the sixth day, it happens again. So, six days have passed. What do you think they are doing behind the walls of Jericho all this time? They are getting very nervous and more fearful. They don't understand what the Israelites are doing? What is Joshua's strategy? It doesn't make sense. The troops guarding the walls against Joshua start losing their resolve. They are being worn down. They are being confronted with something that they can't figure out. Something had to happen psychologically in the minds of those defending Jericho. The enemies of Joshua were mentally and emotionally broken down, little by little.

Now comes the seventh day, and instead of coming out at their regular time, Joshua and his army come out earlier in the morning. The enemy recognizes this is different and it unnerves them even more. God gave Joshua another "new" instruction. Instead of walking around Jericho once, the army is to walk around the walls seven times. That must have taken awhile. Imagine walking around a whole city seven times. At the end of the seventh time around, the seven priests who had accompanied Joshua's army were told to blow their trumpets. At the same moment the trumpets sounded, Joshua and his army began to shout—all 40,000 soldiers. The people behind the walls were scared out of their minds. They didn't know what was coming. They felt surrounded. It was intimidating.

Why didn't God just do that in the beginning, on the first day around the walls? Because it's part of war; it's part of the covert strategy. In order to defeat an enemy, you must first create conditions to foster doubt and break their confidence. Time and time again in the Old Testament, this is how God led His people to victory over their enemies, sometimes without ever having to enter into combat with them.

But in the story of Joshua, one element is very critical for you to know to help you see how the spiritual realm is always paralleling the physical realm. Before the walls fell, ***preceding*** the troops, the Ark of the Covenant was carried before them. Who is the Ark of the Covenant today? In the last verse of Chapter 11, in the Book of Revelation, it states:

> ***"Then God's temple in Heaven was opened, and within his temple was seen the Ark of his Covenant."*** Revelation 11:19

And then, Revelation, Chapter 12:1 follows:

> ***"And a great sign appeared in the sky, a woman clothed with the sun, with the moon under her feet and on her head a crown of twelve stars. She was with child***

> ***and wailed aloud in pain as she labored to give birth."*** Revelation 12:1-2

The Ark of the Covenant, the Woman who contained God in Her womb, the Queen, the "Big Q," Our Lady—and She came in 1981, ***preceding*** all the events leading up to this moment, all the while dropping Her intel, Her messages, from Heaven. **These messages are your secret code. It is what you need. It is how you are going to conquer evil.**

Our Lady told us on November 2, 2014:

> **"...My Son promised me that evil will never win..."**

The story of Joshua speaks to us even further. **Seven** priests led the army, for **seven** days, and on the seventh day, they circled around the walls **seven** times—**7-7-7.*** This is just another **"intel drop"**

* The 7-7-7 prayers consist of 7 Our Father's, 7 Hail Mary's, and 7 Glory Be's. These prayers were the first prayers that Our Lady requested the six Medjugorje visionaries to pray every day. Our Lady told them to pray these prayers for the intention of peace.

from Heaven, if you want to put it into worldly terms, that helps us understand and digest what Our Lady wants to communicate in the spiritual realm and how it connects to the physical realm. "The" Ark of the Covenant told us on March 21, 1988:

> **"...Pray, dear children, and your Mother will pray with you to defeat satan..."**

We are shouting out our prayers to Our Lady, that She will go to God to knock down the walls our enemies have been hiding behind. The Ark of the Covenant preceded the soldiers in the attack of Jericho. The Ark, the **"Q"**ueen, is preceding us —and through almost 40 years of prayer—has prepared us for this battle. Her purpose is not just to unnerve and defeat our enemies, but to bring them to the fear of God and to conversion. We have something playing out in front of us that is very, very profound.

Two Americas are clearly manifesting themselves; one growing in Light and one growing in darkness. A vaster and deeper abyss grows to separate the two. It is evident everywhere. As Our Lady's children, it is up to us for the Light to prevail through the instituting of Her messages in our lives, our work, our institutions and our nation. This is what it will take to make the transformation of our nation, a transformation that is at hand, toward the Light, which will envelope and overwhelm the darkness, reuniting the "United States" of America in keeping God's law. We hold the "keys" to peace. **[21]**

A Friend of Medjugorje
Two Americas 2004

CHAPTER NINE

A Physical Manifestation of Light vs. dark

As previously stated, fifteen days after the 100th Anniversary of Our Lady's Fatima apparitions of October 13, 2017, Little Q dropped his first "crumb."* The date was October 28, 2017. What did Q title this first entry? "The Calm Before the Storm." A few days later on November 1, 2017, he writes this:

> *"How many military generals have been in and out of the White House in the past 30 days?"*

* Q calls his intel drops "crumbs." Those doing Q Research collect the crumbs or, in other words, the pieces that form a larger picture. When the picture begins to emerge, the results are shared among different message boards, youtube sites, Twitter and Facebook, etc., so that all Qanons — the anonymous army of Q, can partake of everyone's research finds.

> *"What cash payments occurred by Obama during the last 90 days of his presidency to foreign states or organizations?"* [22]

In fact, on the very day Obama was leaving the White House, January 20, 2017, **the very day** of Trump's Inauguration, Obama sent a $221,000,000 check to the Palestinians.[23] If you are a U.S. military general and a patriot who loves the United States of America, what are you going to think about this? What are you going to do if you suspect treason is taking place at the highest level? What do you think these generals would say to President-Elect Trump as he comes into the Office of the Presidency? What would Trump say to the military? And if you are an enemy to America, and you had eight years in the President's office, would you not fill the Federal Bureau of Investigation (FBI) with people who viewed America in the same way you did? Would you not fill the Central Intelligence Agency (CIA) and the National Security Agency (NSA) with your people? *Think for yourself. Reason.*

The Deep State, the bureaucracy, is filled with strategically placed people in all the agencies that Obama and his cronies wanted to control, with people of their own thinking. Would you not hire people, even right before you left office, who would work to subvert the in-coming President's agenda and place obstacles to hamper his administration's ability to function? Trump has been fighting obstructionists for two-plus years. Which means they are fighting all of us who duly elected Trump to the Office of Presidency. They fear the loyalty towards the President, therefore, getting rid of Trump is not enough. As much as they are against Trump, they are against us just as much—the masses. They fear us. They know if we have a good, strong, decisive leader as a center to unite around, like we have in Trump, they cannot crush us. They must crush Trump in order to crush us. This is a physical manifestation of Light vs. dark. This is why Our Lady said, as already quoted:

October 2, 2018

"…conquers evil which is all the more visible…"

But in this moment, evil's agenda is being forced out into the Light. Add all these equations together:

1. October 5, 2017
2. The month that ends the 100th year of satan's reign
3. Trump meets with more than 20 generals, the brightest, the strongest strategists of war in the world.

This is no small matter. See the picture on picture pages 4A–5A in the color section of the book, of the meeting with all the generals. A short-notice call for a meeting does not fit the equation that they were called to the White House for a picnic or a Meet-and-Greet.

On October 31, 2017, **'Q'** posted these questions in his thread: [24]

1. *What is the one organization that isn't corrupt? (the military)*
2. *Why does the military play such a vital role?*
3. *Why is the President of the United States surrounded by highly respected generals?*
4. *What authority does the President of the United States have specifically over the Marines?*
5. *Why is this important?*

Q makes you think for yourselves, to look at the news, to research, to find your own answers and conclusions, to be watching for what manifests. He doesn't often give direct answers, but leads you to the answers through the questions he poses and the links he provides. Q has a worldwide following of his messages or intel drops. The movement has grown into a profound phenomenon. Big Q has been leading by Her intel drops from Heaven since 1981, **literally,** amassing hundreds of millions of followers from all over the world over the past nearly 40 years. It is a strategy that works, as Little Q is finding out. Big Q says of Her Intel from Heaven:

October 25, 1988

> **"... Pray that you may comprehend the greatness of this message..."**

You have to think and pray to crack open the code of Heaven's intel drops to understand the importance of what Big Q is saying. It's bigger than we can grasp, as the following message shows from Our Lady:

April 4, 1985

> **"...I wish to keep on giving you messages, as it has never been, in history, from the beginning of the world..."**

There are more parallels with Big & Little Q that are striking. Joan of Arc was trained by Heaven to enter battle at the age of **17** where through her leadership, and the collaboration of **her generals**, she ended the **100 Year War** and France was saved from extinction. In the year **2017,** as Joan of Arc did in her time, Our Lady does in our time—She comes to end the **100 year reign of satan.** And as Joan of Arc did, Our Lady gathers together, through Trump, the nation's **faithful generals** to carry out Her orders. What is at stake in this battle? As with France, the elimination of the United States of America as we know it. Coincidence? It cannot be.

France was down to a few square miles before Joan appeared on the scene. We were down to a very thin thread holding our nation from falling, that could have so easily snapped away any possibility of saving the United States had Clinton won. After posting those questions on October 31 (you may want to reread them again on page 77), Q writes the following day, on November 1, about Trump winning the election the year before and the controversy that arose with the votes from the electoral delegates. If you were paying attention, you may remember at that time, the Democrats wanted to recount the electoral delegates.

You may also remember feeling very disturbed, if you know your enemy, because it was obvious that if they recounted the electoral votes, they were going to commit fraud and hand the election to Hillary Clinton. There was no other reason for a recount but to steal the election. Trump would lose. But, according to Q, the military was watching this closely. They knew what was happening and they were making a plan. Here is what Q says concerning that moment:

> *"If Trump failed, if we failed and HRC (Hillary Clinton) assumed control, we as patriots (the military) were prepared to do the unthinkable."* [25]

That's a big statement. What was the unthinkable? What was Q speaking of? The military was watching this attempt to make a recount of the votes, which would end up putting Clinton in office. So, according to Q, the military was ready to act to stop it. That would be "the unthinkable" to Obama. Keep in mind the military takes an oath to *"support and defend the Constitution of the United States against all enemies, foreign and domestic, that I will bear true faith and allegiance to the same; and that I will obey the orders of the President of the United States and the orders of the officers appointed."* But Trump wasn't President yet. Obama was still President at that point, so the military was still underneath Obama's authority as Commander and Chief, right? But Q seems to be inferring that when it came to allegiance, the military was aligning themselves with Trump over Obama? Why?

We have to go back in time to see how this allegiance for President-Elect Trump could have developed.

"When once a republic is corrupted, there is no possibility of remedying any of the growing evils but by removing the corruption and RESTORING ITS LOST PRINCIPLES; every other correction is either useless or a new evil." [26]

Thomas Jefferson

CHAPTER TEN

"Logical Thinking Required"

In the 1990s, there was a military parade organized in New York City. But what happened at this parade was shameful. The parade was so poorly organized that there were no people lining the streets to honor the Veterans, nor were there any police there to protect them or control traffic. When these Veterans came to a red light, the traffic didn't even stop. Cars ran right through them. It was a shameful act, a display of indifference, and lack of respect for these American heroes.

Donald Trump learned about what had happened and what a disgrace it was He organized another parade. He promoted it, publicized it, and got the people out to support the Veterans. Amazingly,

1.4 million people came to watch it. It was a huge success.

After the parade, an admiral called Trump and said he would like to meet him. The admiral didn't ask Trump to come see him. The admiral went and met with Trump and said that he was representing the Joint Chiefs of Staff, relaying that they were very appreciative of what Trump did for the military and for our Veterans. They wanted to invite Trump to come to the Pentagon.

Trump later flew to the Pentagon, and when he walked into a room where all the generals were gathered, he was impressed. Trump said he never saw so many generals in one place, all the way from the top to the bottom—Four Star Generals down to One Star Generals. In their meeting, they again expressed how appreciative they were to him for what he did for the Veterans. They then stated that they wanted to share some things with Trump.

It is not known what they divulged to him, but Trump came out of the meeting deeply convinced that nobody will ever be able to conquer the United States of America from the outside.[27] A strong nation unites when attacked. However, when the attack is from the inside, as the Deep State is, the nation will topple if it is not surgically removed. It is believed that Trump's relationship with the military continued to develop through the years, and some people speculate that they even asked him to run for President. Fast forward to the 2016 presidential race. Just when Trump is declared the new President of the United States, there is an immediate move to invalidate the results of the election. The Democrats are insisting for a recount of the electoral votes. Here again, as already quoted, Q states on November 1, 2017:

"If Trump failed, if we failed and HRC (Hillary Clinton) assumed control, we as patriots

(the military) were prepared to do the unthinkable." [28]

Meaning what? Meaning that the military would take action. That is unthinkable. So, what did they do?

Q states that information was purposely leaked internally, so that it would get to Obama, as to what the military was prepared to do to stop this attempt of what, in full reality, would have been a coup. As a result of this leak, there was 'a stop' put upon the electoral delegate recount scam which aimed to put Hillary Clinton into office. If this information is accurate, it is very profound. If you remember, during that time, when the news was reporting that Clinton's people were pushing for a recount, suddenly the story just dropped. Q added in his November 1, 2017 post, concerning the leaking, that if there had been a move to recount, there would have been consequences:

Q: *"There is simply no other way than to use the military. It's that corrupt and dirty [the Deep State]. Please be safe and pray for those in harm's way as they continue to protect and serve our great country. Let these coming days be remembered in our history as a time we fought to recapture the Republic from those evil, bad actors who for so long have sacrificed the good peoples' land for their own personal gain. Fight the good fight. Let Justice be served."* [29]

What we are seeing is a purifying of the government. That is not going to just happen. It is what Trump has been working on from the moment he got into office, of what he had mapped out in a speech on October 13, 2016, charting out a plan three weeks before he became president. Q reported, presently, in the Department of Justice alone, there are 470 attorneys who have been charged with the duty of uncovering the Deep State corruption. There are reportedly more than 82,000 sealed indictments that are pointed to individuals from all 50 states. [30]

To be "indicted" means a case has gone before a Grand Jury, who concluded that there is reasonable likelihood that the suspect committed a crime and should be brought to trial. A "sealed indictment" accomplishes the same thing, but is done in secret, so the offender doesn't know he is about to be arrested. In fact, a sealed indictment will prevent the suspect from even discovering that he is being investigated. This reduces the risk of a suspect fleeing. So, with more than 82,000 sealed indictments (and counting) waiting to be brought to trial, is this the coup d'état? [31]

We do not know, but we do know we are in a spiritual realm of both, between Heaven and hell, which is being acted out in the physical realm between the children of Light vs. those of darkness. Q continually reassures his followers, this is planned to happen in the future. That sounds like something from October 5th. One other interesting piece of information is that the indictments began in the same month that Q began to post—October 2017.

If you have people, who are in public office, undermining the power and authority of the United States, that is treasonous—and can send people to prison for life, or high treason can receive the verdict of capital punishment. It is well known, with the facts to prove it, that the Obama's and the Clinton's and others have committed what may be actions of high levels of treasonous acts. Q states that Trump has all the evidence against them and all the Deep State operatives and is waiting for Mueller's investigation on him to end before he begins exposing the evil agendas of the Left. There are a lot of names that are involved, as well as those in government positions of other countries. Again, according to Q, Trump is waiting to make the move. Why?

Q reveals why in a post on November 9, 2018. He writes:

> *"Logical thinking required."*
>
> A. *How can arrests occur prior to removing the corruption from the DOJ (Department of Justice) and FBI?*
>
> B. *How can arrests occur prior to safely securing a majority of the SUPREME COURT [CONSTITUTION – RULE OF LAW]?*
>
> C. *What is the role of the Senate?"* [32]

Think. Reason. Research. There has to be strategy on both sides, speaking of the spiritual realm that plays out into the physical realm. What is that strategy? One Q analyzer explains it this way:

> *"In the game of chess, for example, you don't get to make two moves in a row, you move your piece and then your opponent moves their piece but you never know if your op-*

ponent is going to take three seconds, three minutes or 30 minutes to make his move. So, you have to wait for your enemy to decide his strategy, what move he will make. Once he moves, you can move. There are a lot of holds and pauses by Trump who is strategically, waiting for the enemy to make his move, before Trump makes his next one." [33]

Typically, you make a move and then your enemy makes a move. When it comes time to make a second move, you are forced to reveal more of your strategy. Your opponent can then more effectively counter you because he understands your battle plan better. To completely conquer your opponent, you look for that one move that will sweep him off the board; a checkmate. Otherwise, the more the game continues, the greater the chance the enemy will find a way to checkmate you. Trump is smart, looking to the military generals and getting them involved.

One question to ask: Is Trump giving an appearance to make the enemy think they are in control? A disinformation operation? The October 5, 2017, meeting with the generals, showed that Trump has the military aligned with him. Is there a whole strategy playing out behind the scenes? Obviously, before the country can be purified, all the corruption that stems from enemies of our nation must be indicted—a difficult task to accomplish when the agencies responsible for this are themselves corrupt. If there are 82,000 sealed indictments that will be opened, it is going to be comparable to a military type operation. Just like when the Normandy invasion freed France, a plan coming out of nowhere to completely purify the government parallels also Our Lady's plans. Our Lady, Big Q, said on July 25, 2017:

> **"... Be prayer and a reflection of God's love for all those who are far from God and God's Commandments...be...determined in con-**

version...on yourselves so that...life may be truth...so that your life on earth may be more pleasant..."

Corruption always prevents life from being pleasant.

Medjugorje is the event, a time given to Our Lady that has been in waiting for 2000 years, even foretold in Genesis, "the woman will crush the head of the serpent"—one of the most displayed acts of God's love, outside of Jesus' life, in the history of man. You, as an individual, are chosen to be used in this plan. A plan so important, so big you cannot fathom how great your role is in God's design. You can only pray to find out what your role is in God's plan. It is the plan. It is a "great" plan for the salvation of mankind. [34]

Friend of Medjugorje
Twenty Years of Apparitions
2001

CHAPTER ELEVEN

Set Our Sights on the Brightest Star

The Medjugorje event is a guarantee. We will be watching, in real time, the entire world being set free from a great amount of corruption. This is Our Lady's time. Our Lady is here to change the direction of the world, and it can't change, as stated in the beginning, until the United States changes. What we will see happen is the whole world being set free from corruption because as the United States goes, so goes the rest of the world.

Several years ago, while I was speaking about separation, everyone was saying we have to talk across the aisle to our enemies. I was advocating the opposite, saying, "no," we need to separate. The early Church did that and this is exactly what is happening now. The more we separate, the more those on the side of darkness become visible as to who they really are and what they stand for. Also, those on the side of Light become visible as to who we really are and what we stand for. Darkness has kept the two sides amalgamated together, and we were led deeper into darkness because we allowed them to dominate us. However, separation will bring unity. How does that work? Because it evolves down to two opposing sides; one side will become stronger and conquer the other. Our Lady said, as stated earlier:

November 2, 2014

> **"...my Son promised me that evil will never win..."**

We will win by the "intel" that is coming from Heaven and by the strategies that are happening now, physically. We are headed to a showdown and it's really exciting because these revelations the

"Big Q" is dropping is intel from Heaven—the spiritual realm, and the "Little Q" intel drops help us to understand the physical realm, and both are playing out. Our Lady said on November 6, 1982:

> **"...Go on the streets of the city, count those who glorify God and those who offend Him..."**

The numbers of the Light are diluted, being among those who offend God. Therefore, those on the side of Light are being united together, spiritually and physically. Our Lady said:

February 2, 2019

> **"...my children, you are not united by chance. The Heavenly Father does not unite anyone by chance..."**

There is a spiritual pressure to get souls of the former so as to identify who is who. Our Lady's words above say everything. So Q and his army are circling the Jericho walls. Are the enemies being made nervous by Q's intel drops, exposing their evil? These darkened souls are realizing that they are being exposed and that they have nowhere to hide among the Light. They are unsettled and they are becoming desperate. Trump and his people have let them think the enemy is in control, but the realization is hitting the enemy that the truth is, they are not in control. This is just how God works things; overnight things can flip. We are being united, not by chance, but by design; the apostles of Our Lady and the "actors" who are in key positions to lead the world to what Q calls "the Great Awakening."

There were many powerful things Trump said in the State of the Union Address. One in particular was very profound. He said, three times, **"This is the time."**

> *"<u>This is the time</u> to unite America. <u>This is the time</u> to search for the tallest summit...<u>This is the time</u> to reunite America."*

Those are Our Lady's words that She has spoken often through the years. That is what She is here for. Trump is one of Her instruments. He is calling for it. And this is Her time. This is the time to unite America. The second sentence in the State of the Union Address says:

"This is the time to search for the tallest summit."

What is the tallest summit? A summit is a mountaintop. The Jews were always called to the mountaintop. Trump then adds:

"...and set our sights on the brightest star."

Who is the Bright Star? Who is the Brightest Star in Heaven? It is Our Lady.

That Star comes down from Heaven every day. To do what? *"To rekindle the bonds of love."* What does Our Lady say? Remember, She said on February 2, 2019:

> **"...My children, you are not united by chance..."**

She said on November 2, 2016:

> **"...The united love of my apostles will live, will conquer, and will expose evil..."**

Our Lady of Medjugorje is the Brightest Star. Why did Trump say what he said? Read it again, think about this, meditate. What do you think this comes from? You think it's by chance? **"...Nothing is by chance..."** [September 2, 2016]

President Trump said:

> *"This is the time to search for the tallest summit and set our sights on the brightest star. This is the time to rekindle the bonds of love and loyalty that link us together as neighbors."*

What do you think about that? This crass guy that people say, *"I don't like his tweets; I don't like what he says."* You can't deny what he just said. There is a link. He's talking about love of neighbor, the bonds of loyalty. That is the purpose of true defeat of our enemy—their conversion. That is the true victory and that is our goal, to conquer them and convert them—that love of neighbor who can be our enemy.

The lead pilot of the massive attack on Pearl Harbor in World War II, Captain Mitsuo Fuchida, delighted in burning to death and killing several thousand U.S. soldiers in a non-declared war. It was a dastardly, cowardly act. Decades after the war, the Japanese pilot converted and became Christian. Many World War II veterans could not forgive him.[35] When you see your friend burned to death and 90% of your own body is burned, it is understandable that they would have difficulty in forgiving.

Make no mistake of what is being stated here. We must conquer and crush the enemies of this nation who are bent on destroying our nation. But, if we are to fulfill our calling as Our Lady's apostles for Her Son, we must—not maybe—we must strive to win over our enemies after we defeat them. We must forgive and love our enemies in the hope of leading them to the Light. None of Our Lady's children wish anyone to go to prison, but in the end, prison has brought about repentance and conversion, resulting in the salvation of many souls.

Medjugorje has everything to do with the dream of our forefathers being fulfilled; to have a nation at peace with nature's God, which made it great. Our Lady states on August 25, 1994:

> **"...I pray and intercede before my Son, Jesus, so that the dream that your fathers had may be fulfilled..."** [36]

A Friend of Medjugorje
Something in the Air
2005

CHAPTER TWELVE

Why?

Why must we forgive and strive to win over our enemies? Because this is Our Lady's time. Whose time? The Brightest Star who has come to restore unity. What does She want to reunite? America, back to the Founding Fathers, and the Christian principles from which it was birthed. We are living in momentous times, just as Trump said in his address:

"In this moment, what will you do?"

We will follow Our Lady—the Big Q. In the last words of President Trump's address, he said:

*"We must keep America in our '**hearts.**'"*

Our Lady said on February 2, 2019:

"...I speak to your hearts..."

Trump continued and said:

"We keep freedom alive in our souls."

Again, in the same message of February 2, 2019, Our Lady said:

"...My Son speaks to your souls..."

You think this just happened coincidentally? You have to reflect on these things. It can't be by chance. Our Lady says that it is impossible. On February 2, 2019, Our Lady spoke about loving your neighbor and about being united, not by chance, and then in the same message, She said:

"...My Son speaks to your souls. I speak to your hearts..."

Three days later, after Our Lady gives the above message, Trump says:

"...This is the time...This is the time...This is the time...the Brightest Star,"

Ending with:

*"...America in our **hearts** and freedom alive in our **souls**."*

Our Lady is here, heart and soul, in this time, to rekindle the bonds of love, through Her apostles who are united and who are called to live and to conquer and expose evil. We are in a moment of greatness. That is how Trump ended his speech. He said:

"Choose Greatness."

Who is great? God is great. Choose God. He exists. He is truth. Our Lady said:

June 16, 1983

"...God is truth; He exists..."

Many, many lies barrage you throughout the day. Identify their voices. How? Think for yourself. Look at everything from a Biblical point of view and the view Our Lady's messages give you. And do what Our Lady said:

February 2, 2018

"...do not believe lying voices..."

"We owe a lot to the Obamas. They helped us. You don't call a plumber for a dripping faucet. You call a plumber for a broken pipe. Had McCain been elected President, he would have become a dripping faucet and continued us on a slow decline, repairing nothing. Obama was a broken pipe, flooding our homes, drowning the whole nation with a stopped up sewer system. Trump, the blue collar billionaire plumber, was called upon to fix the pipe and clear the sewer line to drain the swamp. Thank you, Mr. Obama and Mrs. Michelle, we owe you great gratitude for having riled us up, uniting and motivating us to elect a new founding Father for a Rebirth of Our 'C'ountry."* [37]

A Friend of Medjugorje
Speaking on the Birthday
of our Nation
July 4, 2018

* Riled means aroused to impatience or anger; irritate; agitated; upset

CHAPTER THIRTEEN

Separation For Unity

Many are distraught because of the division in our nation. No one can adequately explain how to fix the divisions. If you pray for wisdom, you will discover the greater the division, the greater the unity. Sounds like a contradiction? The following was written for the opening of Our Lady of Victory's School, the school of the Community of Caritas in Alabama, in September 2017. This is a one room school house that has witnessed to thousands of people how youth should be educated. There is not a school like it in the United States. Every year, the school has a theme. The theme for the 2017-2018 school year was focused on the peril that our nation faces in our time, the division within it, and the path to healing. The following requires thinking, reflecting and reasoning of why "separation is good." Read slowly, thoughtfully and penetrate each word.

Separation is Good

The first step seeds division;
a breaking apart of many fractions and ways;
farther and farther they grow from each other.

The great separation begins to build alliances with other fractions,
slowly the great separation begins to unite multiple groups
to out power other groups.

The group fractions unite under
the principle they must gravitate toward,
involuntarily, joining together, to become more powerful.
They become more 'one' in propagating what they represent.
From hundreds of different group fractions,
separation begins to diminish their numbers.
Unity of purpose begins to form these many bodies
into lesser and lesser group fractions.

The inescapable principle unwritten,
always active, moves everything towards a destination they know not;
yet they know and feel its time begins to arrive.

The moment comes out of hundreds
when the great division whittles down to only two groups,
two fractions of which the inescapable principle delivers them to.

Welcomed or Unwelcomed, it arrives.
The side of Light.
The side of darkness.
Love vs. hate.

This principle, throughout history, time and again,
goes around and comes around to divide and unite man.
Never in history are there so many numbers of people
who will be crushed, pushed, forced into two opposing groups.

A time of the witnessing of both groups whose stars will show
their Light or darkness to attract and complete the separation for unity.
One will lose.
One will prevail.

The one, who appears to be the weakest,
will grow to be the strongest and will win.

There will arise a new people, a new world, a new kingdom,
confounding all those in the dark
because darkness had the power to bring them before the assembly
and have them martyred, both in life and by death.

Yet they will grow into a kingdom
not out of armies and boundaries of land,
a passing into the courts of the kingdoms of the earth, unencumbered,
Their belief will spread like air everywhere, unstoppable.

These people will be in every breath one takes
and consume the whole world.
Our Lady's plans develop not by blue prints,
rather by boots on the ground.

Cognition of real life experiences will bring about a time,
a time of Mary,
transitioning at this moment to a time of choice,
a time of election, a time of selection.

Choice

Election

Selection

These three elements that bring about the unity,
are brought down to two groups,
both sides knowing who will win this battle.
The nation of the Boot, who arose and was empowered,
Who was the greatest in the world,
fell not by the sword, but by the heart.

The seeds of division brought to Rome by
only a few began the separation.
The Roman Empire, by the middle of the 1st century,
consisted of one thousand Christians.
The Roman Empire, around 100 AD,
Consisted of seven thousand, five hundred Christians.
By the 300 AD, there were six million Christians.
By 350 AD, the Roman Empire of sixty million,
Consisted of thirty-three million Christians.

The blood of the people of the Cross,
of the Country of the Boot,
its gentiles became,
with all its growing branches across the world, united to the vine,
gave life, dominated and conquered the Roman Empire.
Its tree produced a fruit of division that united the world before
and will now again in this time achieve the same.

What is martyrdom?
It is defined by witness,
answered by the call to separate for unity,
following the heritage of the Country of the Boot,*
The people of the Boot,
asked into being by the Lady of this time.

You are chosen.
You are elected.
You are selected.

* This, of course, refers to the country of Italy. Rome was the heart of the Roman Empire. It was in Rome that Peter and Paul were sent to spread Christianity, and through their witness, the Faith spread throughout all of the pagan Roman Empire.

You are the Caritas Community,
Elected to change the whole world
By the call in that faithful month of October*
Witness by your life.

A Friend of Medjugorje
September 28, 2017 AD

Again, thanks to all you who have disenfranchised us. You polarized and strengthened us, who yearn for the Light. You will see that Light will be birthed from this darkness. When you find yourselves drowning in your darkness, you can change your heart and join us in the Light. Don't mistake that what is said here is spoken self-righteously. We only claim that we are sinners, like you. Our ranks are filled with those who once walked in the dark-

* A Friend of Medjugorje received a message from Our Lady through Medjugorje visionary, Marija on October 6, 1986. Our Lady told him, **"Pray and by your life witness. Not with words but rather through prayer will you attain what your desire is. Therefore, pray more and live in humility."**

ness. The difference is we repent and we recognize sin in our lives and that we need a Redeemer. That Redeemer is the Light we possess within us that we received by recognizing our sinfulness and then accepting Him in our hearts, through asking for forgiveness. Our Lady said:

May 2, 2009

> **"...Do not permit darkness to envelop you. From the depth of your heart cry out for my Son. His Name disperses even the greatest darkness. I will be with you, you just call me: 'Here we are Mother, lead us...'"**

Are we willing to resist rather than submit? We, the people of our nation; how many are willing to resist? Or rather submit to the demoralization of our nation, our Christian faith, our Christian principles, so long as our jobs, homes, and ourselves are left alone? It is plainly–painfully obvious that we, in this nation of ours and other nations, are unconscious of the choice before us. Resist or submit. We must make our decision now. [38]

A Friend of Medjugorje
Declaration of a Showdown
2007

CHAPTER FOURTEEN

A Recap

After airing the broadcast of February 14, 2019, on *RadioWAVE* Special World Report, in which this topic was discussed, we received the following feedback:

> *"Wow, the last radio show educated your listeners on a full-blown, over the top conspiracy theory. I'm a Field Angel* and am disappointed that you all choose to bring awareness to what sounds like to me lying voices."*
>
> *L.*
>
> *Herndon, Virginia*

To L. and others who may have the same initial response that "Q" is just another "conspiracy

* A supporter.

theory," some thoughts, based in reason, as to why it is important for the followers of Our Lady to be familiar with Q.

1. Nothing is by chance.

2. Whether it is another conspiracy or not, what strikes one is that there are various aspects of truth, while some aspects may need to be rejected. But it serves as a good lesson of what all of Our Lady's children are to do.

   A. Think for yourself.

   B. Reason out events, yourself, prayerfully, by reading the Bible and Our Lady's Messages.

Also, a good method to adopt and also a good example to practice is studying the Chinese War book, "Art of War," written 2500 years ago by Sun Tzu. Our Lord and Our Lady taught us to love our enemies, and to be just with them. Our Lord and

Our Lady said to love our enemies and do good to them. But, Our Lady and Her Son did not say, you are not to understand your enemies. No! You must know your enemies to defeat them.

There are some things authentic in “Q’s” intel drops, which parallel Our Lady’s messages. You have read many in this book. Go back and just read the messages themselves.

Q is a Movement of Resistance

“Q” is much larger than whoever is behind Q. Q started a movement that has lit a fire throughout the nation that is now spreading to other nations. It is a movement of resistance. Q doesn’t give answers; he asks questions designed to make people think. He directs people to “think,” “reason,” “research,” and “dig.” I have been telling you for years to think, don’t just accept what you are told, do your own research. Do a lot of research with the messages to understand what Our Lady is saying and what She desires you to do. She is not saying to stick your head in the sand like an ostrich so you won't see the danger. Our Lady says:

November 2, 2016

"...expose evil..."

She says:

July 25, 1995

"...may good overcome evil..."

You can't overcome evil unless you know what evil is and where it is hiding. You must think, you must reason, and you must look and study everything with prayer.

For you who would take our liberties away unlawfully, we address a question to you: Are *you* willing to go to jail? Are *you* willing to die? We will not be idle while you dismantle our nation and take from us our right to follow our true Liberator. So my call today to those who deny me my right to exercise my belief in following Christ, my Liberator, I say:

Tyrants' reign will always end in disastrous defeat, ours in glory. We willingly give our life, while they unwillingly pay with theirs."™

Friend of Medjugorje

Friend of Medjugorje
They Fired the First Shot 2012™

When Medjugorje visionary, Marija, came to live in a Friend of Medjugorje and his wife's home for three months, over and over again, the Blessed Mother chose to appear in their Bedroom, making a profound statement of the importance of marriage and family. Our Lady appeared to her every day in the Bedroom, except for one day. Thanksgiving Day, 1988, Our Lady appeared out in a Field, near a large pine tree, where years before, a Friend of Medjugorje with his family, consecrated it to God, with the prayer, *"May all who see this Tree, see God in it."* The Blessed Mother chose to appear in the Field on the day that our nation gives thanks to God, for His blessings upon us, our families and

our nation – showing it is through individual conversion that brings healing to families and then to our nation. The apparitions in the Bedroom have come to be known for the healing of the family, while the Tree represents the healing of the nation. Through the healing of our nation, the world will be healed.

(AP Photo/Pablo Monsivais)

Historic Meeting, October 5, 2017

Eight days before the 100th anniversary of the Fatima apparitions, in which the Virgin Mary appeared in Portugal, in 1917, and foretold that Russia would spread her errors throughout the world. It cannot be by chance that President Trump called a meeting on the above date, October 5, 2017, with his top generals, concerning the threats of evil against our nation and the world. As Our Lady foretold in the Fatima apparitions, World War I would end soon, but unless men stop offending God, a larger and greater war will break out. This led to World War II and the many evils that we face today.

On this day, President Trump, speaking to the world's great military leaders, said:

> *"It falls on the people in this room to defend the American people from these threats…I put my trust in you to execute our mission aggressively and effectively…I also expect you to provide me with a*

broad range of military options, when needed, at a much faster pace. I know that government bureaucracy is slow, but I am depending on you to overcome the obstacles of bureaucracy…"

Why did Trump say, "I am depending on you to overcome the obstacles of bureaucracy?" **Chinese warrior, Sun Tzu said,** *"If you know yourself, and you know your enemy, you will win every battle and win the war."* What manifests in the physical realm is a reflection of what is happening in the spiritual realm. Our Lady revealed this to Medjugorje visionary Mirjana on December 26, 1982, when She said:

"…you must realize that satan exists. One day he appeared before the throne of God and asked permission to submit the Church to a period of trial. God gave him permission to try the Church for one century. This century is under the power of the devil, but when the secrets confided to you come to pass, his power will be destroyed…"

October 13, 2017, 100 years of satan's reign ends—100th anniversary of the Fatima, October 13, 1917, apparition and October 13, 2017, the year beginning the century being given to the Virgin Mother, Queen of Peace. Our Lady said in the present Medjugorje apparitions, December 25, 1999, "…**a new possibility for peace in this century is opened…" "this century will be for you a time of peace and well being."**

In the Medjugorje apparition, December 26, 1982, to Mirjana quoted above, Our Lady continues the message, explaining why satan is doing so much damage in th world today.

"…when the secrets confided to you come to pass, his power will be destroyed. Even now he is beginning to lose his power and has become aggressive…he is responsible for obsessions and murder."

This is the moment this is the time.

Weakness shown to ISIS and other enemies, kept the U.S. in battle for the last 16 years. A weak resolve gives rise to third-rate thugs. Trump in nine months has all but obliterated ISIS. The world is in need of moral order. The U.S. is the only country in the world that is able to stabilize the world. If the U.S. ceased to exist in this age, the world would be an inferno. President Trump has prioritized to make America stronger than ever before. That is why he is the most attacked leader in the world. The move to impeach a president by searching for a crime that is not known and creating evidence to do so, is not only illicit, it is a crime. Those purporting to create a case for impeachment, merit charges of treason.

(AP Photo/Carolyn Kaster)

(Above) Monday, August 13, 2018, President Trump watches an air assault exercise, complete with snipers on the ground. Trump signs a new defense bill – "Military intelligence" (The Physical Realm). It is clear there is a great struggle taking place in our nation.

Thursday, August 2, 2018, a Friend of Medjugorje spoke of how the great struggle manifesting today has been hundreds of years in the making. (The Spiritual Realm). Our Lady of Medjugorje said on August 2, 1981:

> **"...A great struggle is about to unfold. A struggle between my Son and satan. Human souls are at stake."**

A Foundation to Last for Centuries

Etched in the eight foot deep foundation on bedrock to support a three quarter million pound Cross, are the words, "For the Soul of America." People have flown in, climbed the mountain to the Cross, to consecrate themselves, their families, businesses and their political office to God.

For a period over 20 years, a Friend of Medjugorje prayed and planned the Cross on Penitentiary Mountain. It is not a symbolic Cross. It is a grace-giving Cross built to consecrate the United States of America to the Cross of Jesus Christ.

On June 30, 2013, Medjugorje visionary Marija climbed to the top of this mountain to give the Cross, through consecration, to the Virgin Mary to heal our nation. Our Lady appeared to Marija facing the people, then turned around to face the Cross and made the Sign of the Cross as She blessed it. Therefore, one should take this Cross seriously, knowing that it was built for the healing of this nation, and comprehend that Our Lady turned to bless it and acknowledge it, on behalf of Her Son. The Cross was built to be an instrument of conversion for this Nation back to God.

The path of the Stations of the Cross, that winds its way up the mountain, through woods filled with Alabama Pines, breaks out onto rough and rocky terrain at the end. Thousands have felt grace from this Cross and have traveled from all over to pray for themselves, their families, this nation and other nations. That is the power of the graces felt at the Cross. This Cross was intentionally built for conversion and the healing of the United States. It's taken 20 years of prayer to obtain the right to build it, meaning, it had to be built spiritually with sacrifices first, giving it what is necessary to dispense graces, then it was constructed physically.

The mystical night that opened the door for the path to our Nation's healing.

See explanation on pg 12A–13A

In 1993—nine–day novenas were begun each month for seven months. The seven novenas were for the Reconciling of Ourselves, Our Family and Our Nation Back to God. With 75,000 people joining in prayer across the nation every year, it amounted into tens of millions of prayers for our nation through the 26 years. Those prayers gave a gift none expected in 2008. The story follows:

Medjugorje visionary, Marija was in Alabama for five days of prayer for our nation leading up to July 4th. During the apparition on the eve, July 3, 2008, at 10:00 PM Our Lady appeared. Our Lady was looking at everyone and listening to those surrounding Her, while all the people recited, in Her presence, the Entrustment Prayer for the consecration of the United States of America into Her hands. The crowd was in awe when, after the consecration, Marija said, *"Our Lady accepted this consecration."*

To understand the significance of that consecration, read here below the words that Our Lady heard from the thousands gathered before Her in the Field, recited to Her. Reflect on the Queen of Heaven taking in each word.

The Solemn Act of Consecration of Our Nation July Fourth, The Year of Our Lord – Two Thousand Eight To You Our Queen, Holy Virgin Mary for this Day of Deliverance

We the people, in Your Holy presence,
who are nothing, appeal to Your Heavenly
Queenly power of intercession before God,
as our Mother.
As such, we Your children appeal
most urgently, most direly with a cry of
lamentation as of the city of Nineveh,
who were a people who humbled themselves
and repented and God relented of His
judgment against them.
We, O Queen, deserve Divine judgment.
We realize that civilizations across time and
cultures who crossed the line of decadence
that we have crossed, all met with their end.
The signs of the time speak to us of our nation.
We have little time left.
We Your children, therefore,
make our plea of consecration at this moment,
giving directly to You this nation,

whose might and glory, we acknowledge,
began and came through being foundationed
on Your Son's, our Savior's, principles.
Through this entrustment, we beg to include
our whole future into Your hands.
Please, at this moment, accept our sixteen
years of novenas, our prayers,
our sacrifices, and heal our land.
We know it starts with our hearts,
so we give You our hearts to heal our land.
May this consecration give into Your
possession this land, that God may
look down upon what is Yours and heal this land.
O Queen, who can we turn to but You?
We look for no other remedy,
with our recourse only to You.
Pray over us at this moment.
Pray over our nation now
on this day of deliverance.
Please stretch out Your arms and
place a seal across this nation with Your
prayers while You are in our midst.
Let this seal be as a sign to the Father.
O Holy Queen, take this consecration,
the ownership of our nation, and
as its Queen, heal this land.
With the dreams of our fathers,
on this day of remembrance of our nation's
birth, think of your Son's birth and
remember not the sins of this land,
but rather how much this nation has dispensed
the liberty of the Gospel to the world.
We bind this nation to the Cross.
Please heal this land.
Lord of our nation, we crown You King,
with Our Lady's hands,
through this consecration
to rule over us, over everything.
Thank You O Mother.
Thank You our Queen.
Thank You for being present.
May Christ grant our nation deliverance
through this consecration. Amen.

A Friend of Medjugorje
Written in Medjugorje,
on June 24, 2008,
for July 4, 2008.

Melania Trump, First Lady of the United States, in a private prayer meeting with 'The' First Lady of the United States, the Virgin Mary, to Whom the United States of America was consecrated to upon its founding by Bishop John Carroll in 1792. Stop and stare. Understand 'well' the signs of the times. We have the First Lady of the Nation that leads the world, in the White House, praying to the Virgin Mary, Mother of God, the First Lady of Heaven. The role of wife and mother is a powerful role, when lived in God's order, as a helpmate to her husband's mission. A wife who does this has her husband's heart…and his ear. So goes the United States, so goes the world. This picture is a message and a sign of hope.

Conservative Political Action Conference (CPAC) Saturday, March 2, 2019 in Maryland.

President Trump spoke for two hours at CPAC. As he comes on stage to Lee Greenwood's "God Bless the U.S.A," he is clapping and lingers near the flag.

Then, just as the song comes to this line, ***"and I'd gladly stand up next to you and defend Her still today."*** Trump decidedly walks over to the American flag, embraces it, rocks it back and forth, says of the flag, representing our Country, "my Baby," and then walks away.

A Jericho tactic: unnerving the enemies behind the walls that Trump is about to "Blow the Trumpets" to knock them down.

March 2, 2019—President Trump is walking on stage, clapping before his talk at CPAC. When suddenly he makes a clear, unmistakable circle in the air and then makes a straight line angled down with his finger. He is making, without a doubt, the letter 'Q' suddenly and very clearly. This is something that Trump has been

doing in his rallies and speeches, more and more frequently as 'Q followers' have been reporting over the past year. They have dubbed it an "Air Q."

After President Trump finishes the Q, he starts clapping, and then makes an unmistakable gesture to say that this was not an incidental happening. He raises his hand and looking directly at the crowd, he points at them as if to say, "Yes. You got it. I did a 'Q'." Some believe the President is Q+ (+ means plus).

"Dear children, today I am united with you in prayer in a special way, praying for the gift of the presence of my beloved Son in your home country. Pray, little children, for the health of my most beloved son, who suffers and whom I have chosen for these times. I pray and intercede before my Son, Jesus, so that the dream that your fathers had may be fulfilled. Pray, little children, in a special way because satan is strong and wants to destroy hope in your heart. I bless you. Thank you for having responded to my call."

Our Lady Queen of Peace, Medjugorje
August 25, 1994

Q Bypasses the Media & Goes Straight to the People

The media wants to control the narrative because they want to **prevent mass awareness** of the deception and injustices being perpetrated over the American people. But Our Lady is here to make us aware of everything. She says on August 29, 1982:

> **"...I am the Mother who has come from the people..."**

The media's hatred of Trump and their collaborative effort to destroy his Presidency, puts him at a great disadvantage. Is it not logical to think that Trump would look for other ways to get the truth out to the supporters who make up his base? Does not the Left use all kinds of disinformation tactics to deceive the public? Is it such a stretch of the imagination to think that some of these same measures could be used to bring truth to the public? If there was nothing authentic to Q's posts, would he not already have been discovered as a fraud? In the above feedback, L. wrote, "*...what sounds like to me lying voices.*" What that sounds like is that L. hasn't done any research on her own. If not, then how can she make an educated judgment?

Who is constantly attacking and trying to discredit Q? What does that tell you?

Q provides links to hundreds of articles and videos from every major news outlet—from television, to newspapers and magazines, to the Internet that are attacking him to discredit and destroy his following. It was the media that began the narrative that Q is a conspiracy nut. Why so much attention given to what is obviously a coordinated effort among those perpetrators of ~~Fake News~~ Lying

Voices to get rid of a singular voice on an obscure website? Q's response to such attacks is to simply state, *"This is what fear looks like."*

Q said on November 4, 2018:

> *"If we aren't a threat, or real, or simply just a conspiracy theory, why the [constant] heavy attacks?"* [39]

This is the motto of the Q Movement. It is the same spirit as *"United we stand, divided we fall."* There is strength in unity. Q, in fact, is calling for unity—and the call goes out, to not only those who are already Trump supporters, but to Independents and Democrats, to come to the side of Light—those who are undecided and those who are not political. Q professes that the hidden deception of those who are leading this nation to destruction is about to be exposed. In fact, it is already happening. One purpose of Q is to educate the public to this evil agenda. As more people come to understand what has been happening, they will join the side of Light.

Revolution begins with:

***1. Thoughts**, which manifest into*

***2. Reasoning** them into a*

***3. Structure**, then into*

***4. Physical manifestation**.*

Thomas Jefferson once stated that "a little rebellion now and then is a good thing." It starts with us. First, a revolution of spiritual revival.[40]

A Friend of Medjugorje
Something in the Air
2005

CHAPTER FIFTEEN

Evil Can't Hide

Q has literally inducted into his ranks an army of intelligence gatherers who are all over the world—a far greater number than the FBI and the CIA put together—and it's completely volunteer. Hence, the evolution of **QAnon**—the anonymous army of Q. Websites on the Internet were created and developed to share among the QAnons what they uncover in their research; a place to share ideas, theories, think tanks, etc. What this means is that those who are working on the side of evil know that the hounds are always on their trail. Evil can't hide. Evil will be and is being exposed. Q often says on his posts, as a warning to the bad actors, *"The world is watching,"* and he is right. As the side of Light becomes strengthened through sheer numbers and unity of purpose, of principles, of love of God, family and country—the side of darkness will begin to fall apart—the center of darkness will not hold together. QAnons have become Joshua's Army, circling and surrounding the enemy, and their presence is having the same effect. Those working on the side of darkness are getting nervous. They want to believe and listen to the ~~Fake News,~~ Lying Voices, but they are left wondering if Trump is really behind Q. In the cat and mouse game, they used to be the cat, but they now know that they are the mouse.

"Form and make prayer groups..."

Is QAnon a Prayer Group?

On July 3, 2012, during the third consecration of the United States of America, in the direct presence of Our Lady through Medjugorje visionary, Marija, in the Field of Apparitions at Caritas, Alabama, Our

Lady gave the answer to the healing of our nation. She said:

> **"Form and make prayer groups through which we will pray for your healing and the healing of this nation** [USA] **to draw closer to God and to Me."**

It is obvious from reading Q's posts that he is a believer. In some of his earliest threads, he declares that there are those whom they are battling who worship satan. Does anyone doubt that this is true? No doubt, Washington D.C. is the seat of satan's power in the world today. Q often quotes from Scripture and calls for prayer. Many of those who follow Q are also believers, and they also quote from Scripture. They often call upon God for His protection and blessing upon our nation, etc. One of the main QAnon sites **(qmap.pub)** has what they call a "Prayer Wall" in which anyone can enter a prayer. Over 13,110 entries (as of March 2019) have been collected there and it grows every day.

Would that constitute a prayer group in Heaven's eyes? The point is that many believers are a part of this movement, and Q believes and professes that a GREAT AWAKENING is on the horizon for our nation. Truth, which is God, will not be accepted without a national revival.

Our Lady is looking to collaborate with those who will bring peace.

Where will Our Lady look for Her collaborators? Do you think She will look only within the Medjugorje world? Only in the Church? Only among Catholics? Only among other Christians? On January 2, 1989, Our Lady said:

> **"...I want to collaborate with you for I need your collaboration. I want you to become, dear children, my announcers and my sons**

who will bring peace, love, conversion....I want you to be a sign for others…"

In the beginning of 2016, we published a book, Medjugorje: Prepare the World for My Final Coming, that was meant to educate the faithful on the importance of participating in the Great Jubilee Year of Mercy that began on December 8, 2015, and would end shortly after the Presidential elections in the United States, on November 20, 2016. The book included a prayer to be prayed throughout the year, knowing that we were at a crossroads in our nation. It was prayed not only in the United States of America, but all over the world. We were asking Our Lady's intercession that Her choice of President would prevail, and defeat the power of darkness. Following is the prayer that tens of thousands of people prayed, along with hundreds of thousands praying the Patriotic Rosary.*

> In this Year of Mercy, we give to you, our Queen, the presidential election in the United States and beg your intercession in choosing the man best capable of seeing the plans of God fulfilled in our nation. We know you said that peace will not come through the presidents, but we also recognize the significance of these next years of your apparitions and who is at the helm of this nation, as president, will have great bearing on all events that will unfold through Medjugorje. Bring to conversion this next president, that his reign will benefit Your plans. We pray for protection over him and ask that You would

* Millions pray the *Patriotic Rosary,* in all 50 States, and around the world. A Friend of Medjugorje, through Our Lady's inspiration, wrote the *Patriotic Rosary,* who prayed it for the first time at Independence Hall in Philadelphia with only a few others in the early 1990's. It immediately captures the hearts and attention of all those who first hear and pray it. It is a powerful prayer for divine protection and mercy for our Nation and for its rebirth.

> lead and guide his heart, to prepare him for the grave responsibilities he will inherit, and the heavy Cross that will be placed upon his shoulders. As You did with George Washington* and Ronald Reagan,** give him supernatural signs of Your Motherly presence, that he will be filled with the confidence of God in leading this nation out of the shadows of death and into an era of peace, a peace that will spread from this nation to the rest of the world.

It is amazing to read that prayer in Light of everything that is assailing President Trump today—and see him remain resolute, relentless and unbending.

* See "American History You Never Learned" pgs. 19–27. For a free copy, call Caritas of Birmingham at 205-672-2000, ext. 315. Or visit **mej.com** and click on "Downloads."

** See Look What Happened While You Were Sleeping™ to learn how Our Lady revealed Herself to Pope Saint John Paul II and Ronald Reagan to bring down Communism, pgs. 444–463 in chapter 17. To get a free copy, visit **mej.com** and click on "Downloads." Or you can order one by calling Caritas of Birmingham at 205-672-2000, ext. 315.

There can be no doubt that a Supernatural Power is supporting and sustaining him. We are still in the midst of the battle, and there is still a great need to continue to pray, sacrifice and suffer for Our Lady's triumph, but Heaven is on the move. All this has been presented to you, concerning Q, to discern to always be on the lookout of where the Spirit of God is blowing.

February 15, 1984

> **"The wind is my sign. I will come in the wind. When the wind blows, know that I am with you..."**

The Spirit of God is working through those hearts who are open to recognizing Him and His works.

"The general principles on which the Fathers achieved independence were…the general principles of Christianity…I will avow that I then believed, and now believe, that those general principles of Christianity are as eternal and immutable as the existence and attributes of God; and that those principles of Liberty are as unalterable as human nature." [41]

John Adams
June 28, 1813

CHAPTER SIXTEEN

The Declaration Of Independence Gave The Legal Basis For The Legal American Revolution In 1776

The Declaration Of Independence Gives The Legal Basis For A Legal Revolution Now

To institute the Restoration of Christian Principles, we must start by going back to America's very beginnings and seek the wisdom of our Fathers who will speak to us from generations long past. We must then foundation our lives, our families and our institutions upon this wisdom so to rekindle and reawaken the dreams of our Fathers throughout this great land. We must all "go back to self school" and reeducate, reform and reacquaint ourselves with the truths of who we are as a people. When was the last time you sat down and read The Declaration of Independence? The Declaration is not just a historical document, it's a locked and unevolving permanent document that holds the key to freedom, giving continued life to every generation unto today. To lose sight of this document is to put our precious freedoms into precarious hands.

The following should be read slowly and carefully and not only understood but learned.

Every corporation in America has a charter or articles of incorporation, which brings the entity into existence. Caritas of Birmingham has one. I.B.M. has one. They also have what are called by-laws for the governance of the corporation.

The articles of incorporation brings the corporation into existence and identifies the corporation's purpose and intent. The by-laws establish its governance. In the case of America's foundation, the Declaration of Independence is the "articles of incorporation" that brought our nation into existence. The U.S. Constitution provides the "by-laws" of our nation and explains how it will be governed. The Declaration of Independence (the articles) cannot be superseded or done away with by the Constitution (the by-laws). There are no clear moral values of right and wrong within the U.S. Constitution because the Founding Fathers had already placed the moral value *in* the Declaration of Independence.

Original Intent [42] and other books relay many points you are reading. Our side of the aisle is weak because we suffer a deficit in our reading and research. We must familiarize ourselves with these truths above and those that follows.

The Constitution is not the foundational document of the United States, rather the Declaration of Independence is the foundational document of our Constitution's form of government. In Article VII, the Constitution attaches itself to the Declaration of Independence. It's very important to understand that the Constitution **cannot be** interpreted independently of the Declaration of Independence, as the Declaration sets forth the "principles" of how the American government would operate. The two documents are not independent but interdependent on each other. The Declaration of Independence had such a continued importance that all the Founding Fathers dated their government acts from the signing of the Declaration of Independence, July 4, 1776, not by the date of the signing of the Constitution.

John Quincy Adams said that the virtues which were "infused into the Constitution" were the principles "proclaimed in the Declaration of Independence," further stating that the Constitution's platform of virtue, its republic character, are from the principles within the Declaration of Independence. Nearly 100 years later, Abraham Lincoln said:

"(Our fathers) established these great self-evident truths that ...their posterity might look

up again to the Declaration of Independence and take courage to renew that battle which their FATHERS began, so that truth...and Christian virtues might not be extinguished from the land...Now, my countrymen, if you have been taught doctrines conflicting with the great landmarks of the Declaration of Independence...let me entreat you to come back... come back to the truths that are in the Declaration of Independence." [45]

What was in Lincoln's thinking, by the above statement? Why does he say to look again upon the Declaration of Independence and to take courage? What was he contemplating in his office when he wrote the above? Study the words carefully and you will understand what he was saying.

Abraham Lincoln was accused of violating the Constitution, he was never accused of violating the Declaration. He admitted that to save the Constitution, he had to violate it. He did so by the principles rooted in the Declaration. Because the Declaration cannot be superseded, Lincoln actually forced the Constitution into an inferior position to the Declaration, using the principles of the Declaration to do it. On one occasion, Abraham Lincoln was confronted by his Secretary of Treasury, Salmon P. Chase, who was objecting to Lincoln and actions he was taking, saying they were in violation of the Constitution. Lincoln's response follows:

> "*Lincoln* (told Chase) *...the story of an Italian captain who ran his vessel on a rock and knocked a hole in her bottom. He set his men to pumping, and he went to pray before a figure of the Virgin Mary in the bow of the ship. The leak gained on them. It looked at last as if the vessel would go down with all on board. The captain, at length, in a fit of rage at not having his prayers answered, seized the figure of the Virgin and threw it overboard. Suddenly the leak stopped, the water was pumped out,*

and the vessel got safely to port. When docked for repairs the statue of the Virgin Mary was found stuck, head foremost, in the hole.

Lincoln (then said), *'I don't intend precisely to throw the Virgin Mary overboard, and by that I mean the Constitution, but I will stick it in the hole if I can. These rebels are violating the Constitution in order to destroy the Union; I will violate the Constitution, if necessary, to save the Union; and I suspect, Chase, that our Constitution is going to have a rough time of it before we get done with this row.'"* [46]

Rebels today are violating the Constitution in order to destroy our nation. We allow it because by stopping the rebels, we think we infringe upon their Constitutional rights. Our nation is being destroyed by foundationless "Constitutional rights"—rights which do not exist. In our time, as in Lincoln's, it is necessary to reestablish the Declaration of Independence and its principles, which supersedes the Constitution, in order to reestablish and save the Constitution.

Look at the dates. The Declaration was adopted on July 4, 1776. The Constitution was signed on September 17, 1787, and not ratified until 1789. Over 11 years later! The Declaration, which most everyone ignores and does not understand what it declares, pre-dates our Constitution by 11 years, 2 months, and 14 days! Yes, our country used the Articles of Confederation in part of the interim, but they did not go into effect until March 1, 1781. Look again at the dates. That is still 4 years, 7 months and 26 days behind the Declaration of Independence. Our Constitution cannot exist without the Declaration, but our Declaration did exist for some time without the Constitution. Therefore, we must always first look to the first document.

The reason our nation has gone astray, is because we began operating solely on the Constitution, without referencing the Declaration. To renew our nation, the Declaration, applying it to today, must be carefully studied for the legal basis of restoring our nation and a basis for a legal revolution. Look to the Declaration, not to the corrupt political processes, for the basis of renewal. The Declaration of Independence, carefully studied, gives a legal basis for a revolution to restore America. Even Thomas Jefferson said:

> *"The tree of liberty must be refreshed from time to time with blood of patriots and tyrants...God forbid we should ever be twenty years without such a rebellion. What country can preserve its liberty if their rulers are not warned from time to time that their people preserve the spirit of resistance? Let them take arms."* [47]

Abraham Lincoln told his fellow countrymen to come back to the Declaration. Lincoln did not say, come back to the Constitution. If it was necessary to do so 100 years after the Constitution was ratified, then why would it be different for us in our present crisis? It is by the craft of satan, with his master intellect, that the courts, over the last 50 years, divorced the Constitution from the Declaration of Independence. The Declaration is the conscience for the Constitution. The Constitution will not hold the course as a stand alone document as the Declaration did. By standing alone as a document, divorced from the Declaration, judges become the conscience of the Constitution, with the Declaration no longer fulfilling that role. This is illegal.

The Founding Fathers foresaw the possibility of this happening and were gravely concerned because even with all the checks and balances they instituted, if judges began overstepping their bounds, it would mean death to the republic. It is in this way that satan is attempting to steal our nation from the Divine Creator who was given sovereignty over the United States of America from its inception. The more Christians will educate themselves and teach their children, their families and their friends these truths, the sooner our nation will be healed.

The prince of darkness, satan, hates a document which first declared independence from an earthly kingdom, England, and then secondly, declared dependence upon God. In this way, the Declaration of Independence was a dual declaration.

Once the preceding is grasped, it can be understood that we have a duty to do what the Declaration states. Read slowly, comprehending and absorbing each word and its meaning.

> *"(The People) are endowed by their Creator with certain unalienable Rights, that among these are Life, Liberty and the Pursuit of Happiness—that to secure these Rights, Governments are instituted among Men, deriving their just Powers from the Consent of the Governed, that whenever any Form of Gov-*

> *ernment becomes destructive of these Ends, it is the Right of the People to alter or to abolish it...But when a long Train of Abuses and Usurpations, pursuing invariably the same Object, evinces a Design to reduce them under absolute Despotism,* ***it is their Right, it is their Duty, to throw off such Government, and to provide new Guards for their future Security...*** "

Go back to our beginning—to the first document of which the establishment of our nation was founded, instituted over 11 years before our present Constitution was drafted and ratified. Lincoln understood that in order to save the nation, we must return to what declared it into being. We must act upon our Declaration to save our Republic.

Our nation and its Declaration of Independence and Constitution have been betrayed and a surrogate system, a third party, has placed itself between "we the people" and the Declaration and Constitution. The surrogate system must be cast out. Something new must rise up by the hand of God, just as Christ rose from the tomb.

We must pray, change our lives and be ready to seize the moment when God grants us the opportunity to completely restore our nation back to its foundation. Signer of the Declaration of Independence, Benjamin Rush, sat next to John Adams in Congress when the Declaration was read. Rush whispered to him if he thought they would succeed in their struggle with England. Adams answered, "Yes—if we fear God and repent of our sins." [48]

Our Lady once said:

November 21, 1983

> **"...It is necessary to make them come back to their promises, which were made at the beginning, and to pray."**

Every school in the nation, every school receiving federal funds has to begin teaching classes, 1st through 8th, with refresher courses in 9th through 12th grades, even memorizing the Declaration of Independence and learning the truth about it. We have grown a population of students in the last couple of generations who believe the opposite. They have moved into and will continue to move into positions of decision-making and through them, we will lose America. A 911 emergency must be made to restructure every curriculum. In fact, we are almost too late. It is not an option. It is mandatory. All immigrants must go through a curriculum of the basics of our nation to become legal, as well as qualify to become a citizen through learning and testing to qualify for citizenship. Otherwise, we will wilt down to what they escaped from and become the same as the nation they fled from. We must go back to what was required and taught in schools from the beginning of our nation for all students and new citizens.

June 23, 2002

> **"My children, I am calling you back to the beginning..."**

To know what to go back to, you must learn what happened in the beginning of our nation. What did the Declaration do? What rights does it give us today? If we do not educate ourselves and our children to the dreams *our Fathers* <u>*had*</u> in the beginning of our nation's founding, they will slip away from us and we will lose the way. Deuteronomy 4:9 says:

> ***"...take care and be earnestly on your guard not to forget the things which your own eyes have seen, nor let them slip from your memory as long as you live, but teach them to your children and to your children's children."***

On the other hand, Hosea 4:6, states:

"My people perish for want of knowledge."

John Adams said:

Liberty cannot be preserved without a general knowledge among the people. We must know our beginnings to determine our future. If we do not, others will determine it." [49]

We let others determine our future when we let Christian principles and faith take the back seat. Noah Webster said:

"The Christian religion is the most important and one of the first things in which all children, under a free government, ought to be instructed...No truth is more evident to my mind than that the Christian religion must be the basis of any government intended to secure the rights and privileges of a free people..." [50]

The following was taken from the book They Fired the First Shot 2012:

John Adams said:

> *"Statesmen…may plan and speculate for liberty, but it is religion and morality alone which can establish the principles upon which freedom can securely stand."* [51]

Adams, in writing again of the Constitution, said that it cannot work if it is put in the hands of immoral and unreligious people. He said:

> *"Our Constitution was made only for a moral and religious people. It is wholly inadequate to the government of any other."* [52]

Meaning: Divorcing the Declaration of Independence from the Constitution leaves an interruptible Constitution document, likened to a ship without a rudder to be blown every which way the wind blows. The ship (nation) can be directed for the protection of unreligious purposes.

Our Lady said:

August 25, 2016

> **"...satan is rolling you like the wind rolls the waves of the sea..."**

Adams wrote that if we allow for the Constitution to be used for protection of immorality and irreligious people, we will lose our liberty. He stated:

> *"The only foundation of a free Constitution is pure virtue; and if this cannot be inspired into our people in a greater measure than they have it now, they may change their rulers and the forms of government, but they will not obtain a lasting liberty. They will only exchange tyrants and tyrannies."* [53]

Our Lady said:

May 25, 1988

> **"...Pray...that satan does not sway you like branches in the wind..."**

"I have embraced crying mothers who have lost their children because our politicians put their personal agendas before the national good. I have no patience for injustice, no tolerance for government incompetence, no sympathy for leaders who fail their citizens.[54]

Donald J. Trump
July 21, 2016

CHAPTER SEVENTEEN

"I Knew This Day Would Arrive" Donald Trump

God Allows Trump's Gleaning*

In the spiritual realm it has been mandated to send Trump through the washer. How is that known? Because "nothing" is by chance. Then what is the reason for it? To set Trump free! For what purpose? *"You will find out!"* Read on for the answer.

How can a real estate magnate work in Manhattan for decades, be scrutinized under a microscope throughout the presidential election and the two years as president and no one has been able to find any blatant or even small corruption? Trump has been gleaned* for the last four years, resulting

* Wrested, exacted, put through the wringer, squeezed, milked, forced, coerced

in nothing being found. Mueller with his highest power microscope, over-the-top probe found nothing. So, why is it said that this attack is mandated from up above, from the spiritual realm? Because its purpose is for the physical realm to thoroughly scrutinize Trump, to show Trump is clean in regards to what his enemies accuse him of. Trump's persecution is a positive because it gives him a clean bill of health, enabling him to go freely after the real criminals throughout our nation's government and agencies. They, the enemies of Trump, will not be able to retaliate against him by hanging something over his head to stop his Normandy Invasion against a massive entrenched Deep State usurpation over the United States government and her people.

Trump is moving into a position to enact what he said he would do three weeks before he was elected President. What you are about to read on the following pages is why Trump said he decided to run for President. **"To make war."** This speech is a revelation that *"this present moment"* is a declaration of war. The speech is worth reading several times. Read it slowly. Absorb his words. Pray to the Holy Spirit before entering into it to illuminate you of what is happening at this moment, that he foretold 2½ years ago.

Donald Trump's Speech—Three weeks before the Presidential Election 2016

On October 13, 2016, the 99th anniversary of the Fatima Apparitions of the Virgin Mary, Donald Trump gave the following speech:

"Our movement is about replacing a failed and corrupt political establishment with a new government controlled by you, the American people. The Washington Establishment and the financial and media corporations that fund it exist for only one reason—to protect and enrich itself. The Establishment has trillions of dollars at stake in this election. For those who control the levers of power in Washington and for the global special interests, they partner with these people that don't have your good in

mind. Our campaign represents a true existential threat like they haven't seen before.

"This is not simply another four-year election. This is a crossroads in the history of our civilization that will determine whether or not WE THE PEOPLE reclaim control over our government. The political Establishment that is trying to stop us is the same group responsible for our disastrous trade deals, massive illegal immigration, and economic and foreign policies that have bled our country dry. The political Establishment has brought about the destruction of our factories and our jobs as they flee to Mexico, China and other countries all around the world. It's a global power structure that is responsible for the economic*

* A global world order. It is not conspiracy. It exists. George H. W. Bush called for it decades ago. [55] Trump is one of the first high profile individuals who have called it out. He, thereby, becomes an enemy to the act of globalization. The antichrist will reign through a "world order". Revelation 13:17, ***"You will not be able to buy nor sell without the mark of the beasts."***

decisions that have robbed our working class, stripped our country of its wealth and put that money into the pockets of a handful of large corporations and political entities.

"This is a struggle for the survival of our nation and this will be our last chance to save it. *This election will determine whether we're a free nation or whether we have only the illusion of democracy, but are in fact controlled by a small handful of global special interests rigging the system, and our system is rigged. This is reality. You know it, they know it, I know it and pretty much the whole world knows it. The Clinton machine is at the center of this power structure. We've seen this first hand in the Wikileak documents in which Hillary Clinton meets in secret with international banks to plot the destruction of U.S. Sovereignty in order to enrich these global* *financial powers, her special interest friends, and her donors. Honestly, she should be locked up.*

"The most powerful weapon deployed by the Clintons is the corporate media, the press. Let's be clear on one thing. The corporate media in our country is no longer involved in journalism. They're a political special interest no different than any lobbyist or other financial entity with a total political agenda and the agenda is not for you, it's for themselves. Anyone who challenges their control is deemed as sexist, a racist, a xenophobe. They will lie, lie, lie and then again, they will do worse than that. They will do whatever is necessary. The Clintons are criminals, remember that. This is well documented. And the Establishment that protects them has engaged in a massive cover-up of wide-spread criminal activity at the State Department and the Clinton Founda-

tion in order to keep the Clinton's in power. They knew they would throw every lie that they could at me, and my family and my loved ones. They knew they would stop at nothing to try to stop me.

"Never the less, I take all of these slings and arrows gladly for you [you the normal Americans]. I take them for our movement so that we can have our country back. I knew this day would arrive. It was only a question of when. And I knew the American people would rise above it and vote for the future they deserve. The only thing that can stop this corrupt machine is you. The only force strong enough to save our country is us. The only people brave enough to vote out this corrupted Establishment is you, the American people.*

* In this age, people were prepared from birth for the battle taking place at this moment.

"Our great civilization has come upon a moment of reckoning. I didn't need to do this folks, believe me. I built a great company and I had a wonderful life. I could have enjoyed the fruits and benefits of years of successful business deals and businesses for myself and my family. Instead of going through this absolute horror show of lies, deceptions, malicious attacks—who would have thought? I'm doing it because this country has given me so much and I feel so strongly that it's my turn to give back to the country that I love. I'm doing this for the people and for the movement and we will take back this country for you and we will make America great again."*

Donald Trump's Speech
October 13, 2016

"Nothing is by chance."

* Only someone with principled patriotic virtues would give up what they had in exchange for what they no longer will have.

Our Lady said She will **triumph**. The man who became president at the most perilous moment of our nation's history was given a name not by chance: **"Trump."** Who is blowing the ~~whistle~~ "**trumpet"** to bring down the Jericho walls protecting the corruption? And who is holding the **Trump card** that is waiting to be played, once the enemies must expose their bluff after showing they are holding nothing of value in the cards they have in their hand?

Melania – A Special Note

Do not discount Melania Trump as not a part of the equation of the events unfolding. She has a part to play in the Holy Virgin's plans that will manifest more and more in the future. Born in 1970, Melania grew up in Sernica, a village near Zagreb, in former Yugoslavia. Her village is only a five hour car trip from Medjugorje. Because of living in a Communist country, Melania's father had her secretly baptized as a child. Sufi mystic Hasan Shushud, a Muslim, prophesied in 1980 that the Virgin Mary would appear in that general area of the world with a plan to save the world. He said that there would be people, especially women, who would be prepared from birth to be a part of Our Lady's plans. He said:

> *"Mary will lead the battle against satan and, co-operating with Archangel Michael, will lead mankind back to God. Mary needs many soldiers for the battle. Each of them will be attracted to the place just in time... These soldiers, most of them women, will be drawn from all over the world. From their earliest childhood they will have been prepared for 'their' special little task, without them having been aware of it."*

Hasan Shushud prophesied this a year before the apparitions in Medjugorje began on June 24, 1981.

This connection a Friend of Medjugorje makes to Melania, came from a friend, Inger Jensen, from Denmark, who met and interviewed Hasan Shushud in 1980, before the apparitions in Medjugorje began. In a visit to Alabama, Inger told a Friend of Medjugorje the story of Hasan's prophecy.

"If you don't know yourself,
and you don't know your enemy,
you will lose every single battle."

"If you know yourself,
and you don't know your enemy,
you will lose every other battle."

"If you know yourself,
and you know your enemy,
you will win every battle
and win the war."[56]

Sun Tzu

CHAPTER EIGHTEEN

T (Target) minus 21 (days) and Counting

On February 26, 2019, Q posted the following Drop:

> It's going to be HISTORIC!
> Planned long ago.
> Within the next 21 days BIG BIG BIG HAPPENINGS are going to take place.
> Q

Q's big announcement has gotten a lot of attention. When we calculated the calendar date from February 26 to plus 21 days, we knew something wasn't just happening in the physical realm, but in the spiritual realm as well. The Target date landed on **March 18th.**

When Medjugorje visionary Mirjana's daily apparitions ended in December 1982, Our Lady promised Mirjana that she would have an apparition, every March 18th, for the rest of her life. Beginning in 1983, Our Lady has appeared annually, as promised. Over time, Our Lady began to reveal to Mirjana that the date, March 18th, is very significant in regards to future events that will take place on that day. Though March 18th is Mirjana's birthday, Mirjana has stated emphatically that Our Lady did not choose that day to appear to her every year because it is her birthday, but because of something that will happen on that day. Also, important to remember is that Mirjana is the visionary to which Our Lady has taught to pray for nonbelievers. Our Lady has taught Mirjana that a nonbeliever or atheist is someone who has never known the love of God. March 18th is a big **"cue"** from Heaven to pay attention to.

As of March 8, 2019, 10 days from the target date, Q has not offered any information about the context of why the up and coming event is

"HISTORIC" and "BIG BIG BIG." Little Q is speaking about the same day that Big Q has spoken to Mirjana about. What we do know is that March 18th is an important day in the future. How soon will something manifest on that date? What we can say is the T-21 announcement countdown falls on March 18th. Every March 18th is significant because it is one year closer to the actual event of March 18th in the future. Each March 18th is a precursor, a sign of things to come. Q's T minus 21 countdown serves, by choosing March 18th, to make more people aware that March 18th is very important.

Friend of Medjugorje

Friend of Medjugorje
March 8, 2019 A.D.

The Recommended Site to Access Q's "Intel Drops"

Qmap.pub

This is not where Q does his posting. We do not recommend that you go to his actual board which is on 8ch.net. It is a dark web with a lot of objectionable images and language on this board. Q chose this avenue to be protected from being forced off other browsers, as Free Speech 8ch.net is a Free Speech board, meaning there are very little regulations covering it. If you go to qmap.pub, you get just Q's drops, but also a lot of other useful information.

For those of you who do not use the Internet, this writing is not an endorsement for you to go towards the Internet. As this book shows you, we will continue to get to you the necessary information and significant developments as they happen.

Endnotes

1. A Friend of Medjugorje, "Darkness is Fighting Against the Light," April 2018
2. Archbishop Angelo Comastri, "*Way of the Cross of Pope Benedict XVI,*" for Good Friday, 2006, from Introduction, Office for the Liturgical Celebrations of the Supreme Pontiff, 3rd Station
3. www.historyonthenet.com/d-day-statistics
4. A Friend of Medjugorje, "Two Americas," 2004, pg. 13
5. The translation of Genesis 3:15 is from the Vulgate, the Latin translation of the Bible, translated by St. Jerome beginning in the year 382. satan has caused confusion over this verse in the Bible. Out of 10 Bible translations, three Catholic and seven Protestant, this verse was changed from "she" to "he" except for in two of the Bibles. For over 1000 years, St. Jerome's translation, as shown above was the official text of the Church, used in the Roman Rite. While some scholarly work is of value; God gave the Bible to man, not to 'modern' scholars who with an attitude of superiority grant authority to themselves to be changers of Scripture. Genesis 3:15 is a perfect example of scholars invalidating and rationalizing the change of "she" to ***"he will crush thy head...wait for his heel."*** The argument scholars use in eliminating "she" is that St. Jerome translated from Hebrew and Greek to Latin, the language of the common man, and that it was a poor translation. Other scholars in the 15th century changed the pronoun to "he" because it was inclusive of both "he and she." Today's modern scholars, to be "more inclusive," are inclined to say, "he or she." Now there are scholars saying the proper translation is neither "he or she," but rather "they." If these scholars are so advanced in their intellect to Gerrymandering scripture, why did the Holy Spirit leave Genesis 3:15, as what was stated at the top of this page, for more than 1000 years? In their arrogance, today's scripture scholars, in essence, are stating that the Church was wrong for over ten centuries, centuries in which the Vulgate influenced the life of the Middle Ages, inspired the Renaissance with its art and architecture, as well as the life and culture of other centuries. This verse is about the Woman, the Holy Virgin Mary, and whether Jerome perfectly translated it from Hebrew and Greek to Latin or not, he (Jerome) had an oral understanding, very close in real time to the inspired writers, which gives even more credibility of knowing "Her" because of living within two or three or so lifetimes from the death of John (John died around the year 100 AD, Jerome was born in 347 AD). So serious was St. Jerome in working on this translation, that he translated the entire Bible within the cave of the Nativity of Jesus in Bethlehem, over the course of 30 years. He wanted to surround himself with the holiness of that sacred place and be influenced by the "Word was made Flesh" as he prayed through his translation, whereas scholars do their work most often in rooms at sterile universities. That the Church has always held the tradition in seeing Our Lady in this Bible passage is self-evident by the many statues and paintings of the Virgin Mary with Her heel standing on the head of a serpent

6. Mark Twain, Joan of Arc, 1989
7. Ibid., pg. 452
8. Ibid., pg 5
9. Ibid., pg. 444
10. https://www.medjugorje.com/medjugorje/scientific-studies.html
11. A Friend of Medjugorje, They Fired The First Shot 2012, pg. 60
12. Q clearance, Wikipedia
13. Ibid.
14. www.evangelical-times.org/20735/gods-providence-and-the-d-day-landings
15. A Friend of Medjugorje, They Fired The First Shot 2012, pg. 112
16. Ibid., pg. 127
17. Qmap.pub
18. A Friend of Medjugorje, They Fired The First Shot 2012, pg. 127
19. Jonathan Cahn, The Book of Mysteries, 2016, Day 15
20. A Friend of Medjugorje, Look What Happened While You Were Sleeping, 2007, pg. 84
21. A Friend of Medjugorje, "Two Americas," 2004, pg. 26
22. Qmap.pub
23. https://nypost.com/2017/01/24/obama-sent-palestine-221m-hours-before-leaving-office/
24. Qmap.pub
25. Ibid.
26. www.freedomkeys.com
27. Donald J. Trump with Kate Bohner, Trump—The Art of the Comeback, 1997, pp. 172-172
28. Qmap.pub
29. Ibid..
30. Pacer.Gov—Public Access to Court Electronic Records.
31. Ibid.
32. Qmap.pub
33. www.prayingmedic.com,youtube, Qanon, February 11, 2019, "Optics Are Important."
34. A Friend of Medjugorje, "Twenty Years of Apparitions, 2001, pg. 55
35. Donald Stratton, with Ken Gire, All the Gallant Men, 2016, pp. 238-239
36. A Friend of Medjugorje, "Something in the Air," 2005, pg. 28
37. Talk given by a Friend of Medjugorje on July 4, 2018
38. A Friend of Medjugorje, "Declaration of a Showdown," 2007, pg. 15
39. Qmap.pub
40. A Friend of Medjugorje, "Something in the Air," 2005, pg. 23
41. John Adams, *Works*, Vol. X, pp. 45–46, to Thomas Jefferson on June 28,1813
42. David Barton, *Original Intent*, Wallbuilder Press, 2005
43. Ibid.
44. Ibid.
45. Abraham Lincoln: *The Works of Abraham Lincoln, Speech and Debates*, Jon H. Clifford, Editor (New York, The University Society Inc. 1908), Vol. III, August 17, 1858, p. 126–127
46. Donald T. Phillips, *Lincoln On Leadership: Executive Strategies for Tough*

Times, Warner Books, 1992, p. 43–44

47. Thomas Jefferson to William Stephens Smith, 1787, Eternal Vigilance is the Price of Liberty, www.freedomkeys.com
48. www.freedomkey.com
49. Ibid.
50. "An American Dictionary of the English Language," 1828 facsimile edition, by Noah Webster. Published since 1967 by the Foundation for American Christian Education, P.O. Box 9588, Chesapeake, VA, 23321, p. 12
51. The Works of John Adams, Second President of the United States, Vol. 9, Charles Francis Adams, Boston, Little, Brown, and Com., 1856.
52. Revolutionary Services and Civil Life of General William Hull, Maria Campbell, D. Appleton and Company, New York, 1848, pg. 266.
53. The Works of John Adams, Second President of the United States, Vol. 9, Charles Francis Adams, Boston, Little, Brown, and Com., 1856.
54. Associated Press, Jennifer Mercieca, "In Acceptance Speech, Trump Embraces Role as Hero of the Forgotten," July 21, 2016
55. http://www.presidency.ucsb.edu/ws/index.php/newworldorder.
56. Sun Tzu, Art of War

About the Author

A Friend of Medjugorje

To look at the events in the physical realm, one must look at what is taking place in the spiritual realm to know one's enemy, to know how to fight, and to know how to protect oneself from Lying Voices. A Friend of Medjugorje has both a calling and a gift of wedding the two together—the physical with the spiritual realms.

Following Our Lady of Medjugorje for 33 years, prayerfully studying Her words, putting them into life, being close to the visionaries and to the events of Medjugorje, and being obedient to Her call, has given him the key to understanding and breaking open Her messages, unlike anyone else in the Medjugorje world. No one has written more on Medjugorje or has entered into the depths of the messages as he has. Being a husband, father of seven children, a successful business man, head of one of the largest non-profits in the State of Alabama, founder of an International mission and an agrarian based community, prolific in his writings in real time and the events of the spiritual and physical realm. He has many best-selling 5-star books that have changed the course of millions of people's lives, a faithful Catholic not afraid to speak truth to error, even to the hierarchy, a very strong Patriot, a studier of history and reader of "good" books—a Friend of Medjugorje brings a wealth of knowledge and life experiences in looking at the events of our day, that literally change lives.

This is why he can speak with such authority, passion, confidence and courage. He has become known for his prophetic insights into the future, based in what he sees in Our Lady's words. He takes no royalties for his writings, as he does not do this for money. All funds from this book goes to supporting the mission.